The brilliance of *UnProfessional* ...
think differently. Jack has uncover...
a great company in today's busine...

—Siimon Reynolds, co-f...
worth \$500 million at its peak

In *UnProfessional*, Jack Delosa has outlined the exact strategies that will enable entrepreneurs to start and build not only the perfect business, but the perfect lifestyle.

—Clair Jennifer, founder of Wombat Boutique and past member of the *BRW* Young Rich List

Jack Delosa's brief and simple guide for entrepreneurs emphasises that they don't need to be a genius programmer like Mark Zuckerberg to achieve success. It can come with attracting the right people, taking a risk and being prepared to move on despite failure.

—Nassim Khadem, *BRW* magazine

Jack Delosa is Australia's leading entrepreneur under 30 and in *UnProfessional* he sums up in very simple steps how you can build the business and lifestyle that is perfect for you. Read this book several times to build your own roadmap to unconventional success.

—Andrew Morello, Winner of the first Australian season of *The Apprentice* and Head of Business Development at Yellow Brick Road Wealth Management

Jack Delosa has been changing lives and helping businesses explode (in a good way) for years, despite his young age. He's taken his extraordinary skills as an adviser, speaker and agent provocateur and distilled them into the one playbook: *UnProfessional*. He's one to watch, and so is this book.

—James Tuckerman, Founder, Anthill Magazine

Jack Delosa helped us achieve rapid growth with Cupcake Central by teaching us how to create a multi-million dollar business, which we have now done successfully. Jack also taught us that challenging the status quo and pushing the boundaries were easier than we first thought.

—Sheryl Thai, founder of Cupcake Central, Winner of the Young Entrepreneur of the Year at The Australian Start-Up Awards

I was a business newbie when I started my business in my spare bedroom and it went on to secure $1.1 million in sales in its first 12 months. Jack Delosa offers top class advice, real-world tips and buckets of inspiration to boot. If you're an entrepreneur who wants to maximise your potential, make *UnProfessional* your handbook to success.

—Lorraine Murphy, founder of The Remarkables Group, Graduate of The Entourage Scalable and Saleable Program

Entrepreneurship is a force that can be used for good. In *UnProfessional* Jack Delosa gives us a step-by-step guide to building something great that just may change the world.

—Samantha Cran, CEO of One Disease at a Time Foundation, listed in 100 Women of Influence by the *Australian Financial Review*

For business owners of any stage, even those yet to start, *UnProfessional* uncovers the key distinctions that will enable you to build a multi-million dollar business the smart way, without killing yourself in the process.

—Stuart Cook, Global CEO of Zambrero, Australia's Fastest Growing Franchise 2011, 2012, 2013 (*BRW*)

UNPROFESSIONAL

UNPROFESSIONAL

JACK DELOSA

How a 26-year-old university dropout
became a self-made millionaire.

And how you can
do the same.

WILEY

First published in 2014 by John Wiley & Sons Australia, Ltd
42 McDougall St, Milton Qld 4064

Office also in Melbourne

Typeset in ITC Garamond Std 11.5/13.5 pt

© The Entourage

The moral rights of the author have been asserted

National Library of Australia Cataloguing-in-Publication data:

Author:	Delosa, Jack, author.
Title:	UnProfessional: How a 26-year-old university dropout became a self-made millionaire. And how you can do the same. / Jack Delosa.
ISBN:	9780730309239 (pbk)
	9780730309246 (ebook)
Notes:	Includes index.
Subjects:	Success in business.
	New business enterprises—Management.
	Small business—Management.
	Business planning.
	Entrepreneurship.
Dewey Number:	658.11

Cover design by Xou Creative, www.xou.com.au

Cover image: © Getty Images / THEPALMER

Social media icons: © Orman Clark. www.premiumpixels.com

Printed in Singapore by C.O.S. Printers Pte Ltd

10 9 8 7

Disclaimer
The material in this publication is of the nature of general comment only, and does not represent professional advice. It is not intended to provide specific guidance for particular circumstances and it should not be relied on as the basis for any decision to take action or not take action on any matter which it covers. Readers should obtain professional advice where appropriate, before making any such decision. To the maximum extent permitted by law, the author and publisher disclaim all responsibility and liability to any person, arising directly or indirectly from any person taking or not taking action based on the information in this publication.

" It is not the critic who counts; not the person who points out how the strong man stumbles, or where the doer of deeds could have done them better. The credit belongs to the man who is actually in the arena, whose face is marred by dust and sweat and blood; who strives valiantly; who errs, who comes short again and again, because there is no effort without error and shortcoming; but who does actually strive to do the deeds; who knows great enthusiasms, the great devotions; who spends himself in a worthy cause; who at the best knows in the end the triumph of high achievement, and who at the worst, if he fails, at least fails while daring greatly, so that his place shall never be with those cold and timid souls who neither know victory nor defeat. "

Theodore Roosevelt, US president, 23 April 1910

This one's for Tom, the biggest unprofessional of us all.

Join the conversation as you read ✓

🐦 #unprofessional @jackdelosa

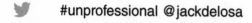 www.facebook.com/australianentrepreneurs

www.unprofessional.com.au/bonuses

CONTENTS

ABOUT THE AUTHOR

Jack Delosa is an entrepreneur and investor who was recently described by *Sunrise* as 'the young Aussie millionaire that didn't finish uni'.

From having one of his companies, MBE Education, listed in the Fastest 50 Start-Ups in Australia, to acquiring businesses with his panel of investors and raising over $10 million, Jack is a leader for future and existing entrepreneurs.

Today Jack's focus is on educating and developing a new breed of entrepreneur through his two business education institutions, The Entourage and MBE Education, which have a combined membership base of 40000 business owners. He also contributed to the development of the curriculum at the Branson Centre of Entrepreneurship in South Africa, helping to educate entrepreneurs where they are needed most.

Jack has spoken for and been engaged as a thought leader for companies such as AMEX, Microsoft, Virgin and CPA on the topic of business growth and performance. Today he is a spokesperson for entrepreneurship in Australia as a regular blogger for *The Sydney Morning Herald*, *The Age*, *StartupSmart* and *Dynamic Business* magazine. He has also been featured in *BRW*, *GQ*, Career One, *Fitness First* magazine, on Channel Seven, Channel Nine, Channel Ten News, *Sunrise*, *The Morning Show* and *Sky Business* and was featured on the cover of *Central Magazine*.

In 2013 Jack founded The Entourage Foundation, a not-for-profit organisation that is igniting a generation of enterprising young people to drive Australia forward by delivering business education nationally through high schools.

In recognition of his successes, Jack has been listed as one of the top 10 entrepreneurs under 30 in Australia in the Dynamic Business Young Guns and in SmartCompany's Hot 30Under30, and four times in Australian Anthill's *30Under30* publication.

Jack's Young Gun blog in *The Sydney Morning Herald* was named in the Top 25 Business Blogs in Australia by SmartCompany.

ACKNOWLEDGEMENTS

First and foremost I'd like to thank Kristen at Wiley for breathing life into this project and being the catalyst for something that will impact the lives of many. Katie, Elizabeth, Fleur and Meryl—you were the hands that made light work and enabled the architecture to come to life, thank you all.

To Steve Pharr for writing a cheque when I was 19 and no-one else would. To Reuben Buchanan for offering a hand up and an invitation to a new world.

To Stuart Cook and Andrew Morello for providing friendship and inspiration since day one.

To Peter Davison for encouraging me to listen to the only voice that matters: you provide *true* mentorship and wisdom that has been very formative for me.

To Matt Church for being a real leader and providing an example of true mastery.

To Justine McKell for seeing the vision and working tirelessly to bring it to life—love ya Jus.

To Jason Williamson for coming on board and rallying an industry.

To Dad for planting the idea that the only things you can't do are the things you can't imagine, and to Mum for providing the unconditional love that would enable such seeds to grow. To Cris for being an example of an exceptional person.

To Anna for having the biggest heart in the world and being you.

To all The Entourage and MBE members, graduates and success stories—you guys are the shining light for so many others around the world that are learning to navigate their own path.

To The Entourage Team, for your commitment to the vision and work ethic to deliver it.

And lastly to Petar, Beau and Josh for being family. It was anthropologist Margaret Mead who said, 'Never doubt that a small group of thoughtful, committed citizens can change the world. Indeed, it is the only thing that ever has.'

The movement marches on ...

FOREWORD

by Dorry Kordahi

Although Jack Delosa's been a friend for some three years, I was genuinely flattered when he asked me to write this foreword for *UnProfessional*, as I know the impact it will have on the lives of so many.

Jack's journey is very similar to my own: we both started young, without inherited wealth and built successful businesses from scratch. Moreover, we were both hungry to learn from others—not in a formal academic sense but from real people who had trodden the same paths we were taking. We both found enormous leverage in our earlier years, in learning from people with 'been there done that' experience.

UnProfessional is the entrepreneurial handbook for anyone looking to start, build or exit a high-growth business and it comes from Jack's experience in his own businesses since the age of 18 and from his entrepreneurial education institution, The Entourage. Through The Entourage, which is today Australia's largest private educator of entrepreneurs under 40, Jack and his team of world-class entrepreneurs educate business owners to accelerate the growth of their business and make more money while having more time to do the important things in life.

Entrepreneurship is a growing trend globally, with the attitude of up and coming generations being very different to the previous generations that would often maintain a 'job-for-life' type approach—an approach that is no longer desirable or realistic.

Of all the businesses in Australia, just 4 per cent employ 20 or more people and only 0.28 per cent employ more than 200 employees. Of course, the upsurge in business start-ups means an equal upsurge in business failures; some statistics suggest that one in three of all start-ups fail in their first year of business—a statistic indicative of the lack of effective entrepreneurial education available in today's fast-changing world.

This book is not just a 'how-to' tome, it is also the very real story of a very successful young businessman telling you what it is really like to start from nothing and realise your dreams. In the pages that follow, you will find not only a lively recount of Jack's successes, but also of his failures. It explains how to embrace your failures, to learn and grow from them, and as Jack puts it, to 'fail forward'—a message I think is critical for entrepreneurs to absorb.

Start-up and early stage businesses need to find a way to stay 'lean' in the early days, to prove or disprove a business model, a new product or a new marketing campaign, without betting the house (literally). This is an important message that Jack manages to get across in *UnProfessional.* He started from a tiny office with two people and I started my promotional marketing company

DKM Blue, now an industry leader, by myself from my parents' backyard garage. In today's business world your customer doesn't care about where you're sitting, they care about what you're delivering.

UnProfessional is of course anything but. In the same way a boxer demonstrates a different flavour of professionalism to a doctor or an accountant, so must an entrepreneur. The business world has changed, the old rules no longer apply and the entrepreneur that wins is the entrepreneur who is truly themself.

Above all else, this book reminds us to have an absolute single-mindedness and sense of purpose that breeds the kind of focus required to be successful in business. Jack echoes the credo of my own book *Power to Act* in that the most important person who believes in you must be you. What you are bad at will always outweigh that which you are good at. You will make mistakes, you will make poor decisions and you will face seemingly insurmountable challenges. Such is the life of an entrepreneur who is required to make more decisions in a week than most people will make in a year.

To be unprofessional is to challenge conventional thinking and innovate your way forward in the hope of creating a better tomorrow. May you use this playbook to your advantage as you invent your tomorrows.

Dorry Kordahi

Dorry Kordahi is the Managing Director of DKM Blue and author of *Power to Act* and co-author of *The Wealth Diaries*. He has been listed in the *BRW* Young Rich List since 2011.

INTRODUCTION

When someone described Virgin as an 'unprofessional professional organisation', Richard Branson said it was just about the best backhanded compliment anyone in business could receive.

To be unprofessional is not to be disrespectful. It is not to be reckless or lazy. It is not to be unpunctual, badly presented or poorly spoken.

To be unprofessional is to be real. It is to create a vision that is not borrowed from the past. It is to develop products that genuinely wow your audience. It is to think of marketing strategies that the management consultants don't have diagrams or buzzwords for yet. It is to think original thoughts and speak of proactive ideas that haven't been documented in the academic playbooks.

It is to question authority, particularly when it is inconvenient to do so. It is standing in front of tradition when the tradition no longer works, but a new way of doing things just might.

While the professionals are constantly striving to prove their superior intelligence, unprofessionals strive to be the dumbest person in the room at all times, understanding that to surround yourself with people who are smarter than you is a wise decision.

While the professionals are planning, unprofessionals are executing in the real world and gaining firsthand consumer insight.

While the professionals are trying to position themselves as indispensable, unprofessionals realise that it is smarter to have a business that runs without them, and work only because they want to, not because they have to.

While the professionals encourage others to follow their lead, unprofessionals are busy creating more leaders to amplify their message.

While the professionals are trying to outspend each other with oversized advertising budgets, unprofessionals prefer to have the media build their brand for them in a way that cuts through the advertising clutter. While the professionals are competing, unprofessionals are forming partnerships that see their brand travel further.

Unfortunately, large corporations, governments and universities have not been able to keep pace with the rapid changes in business over the last 20 years. Gripping their outdated rulebook as if their existence depended on it, these institutions cannot move quickly enough to keep up, let alone stay ahead.

This book is your permission slip to throw out the rulebook, forget the old paradigms and build your business to a position of market leadership using strategies that still haven't found their way onto the notepads of the management consultants.

the dream has changed

Our generation no longer dreams of a career path consisting of attaining good grades, going to university, starting in a junior position and working our way up to retirement on our superannuation at the age of 65.

No longer do we want to follow the antiquated tram tracks of saving up just enough money to put a deposit on a house to become the proud owner of a mortgage that we will spend the next 30 years paying off.

The dream has changed.

Globally, a rising tide of people realise that there is a smarter and far more enjoyable way of building a meaningful life than following the traditional path that has failed so many before us.

Entrepreneurship is growing worldwide. People are realising that in this day and age anybody with a good idea and a lot of drive can take control of their career and commence working on their own project. With minimal investment and some clever tactics to learn lessons quickly and inexpensively, creating a profitable business that provides the lifestyle, income and meaning we all strive for is no longer out of reach.

Whether you are an existing business owner or are thinking about starting your own business one day, in this book I will give you step-by-step information on how you can start, build and successfully manage a multimillion-dollar company without needing to give up your life to do so.

Building a business is a skill, and skills can be learnt. Whether you're searching for that idea or whether you're the owner of a business doing $20 million a year, *UnProfessional* will enable you to accelerate the growth of your business, make more money and work smarter, so that you can live the life you want.

As an entrepreneur you are the architect of your own destiny and, while that may open you up for failure, it also opens you up to a whole new world.

talent is overrated

In 2008 Geoff Colvin, a renowned US journalist, released a book called *Talent Is Overrated*. The book looks at some of the greats of history, such as Mozart, Tiger Woods, Oprah Winfrey, Michael Jordan and Warren Buffett, and asks the question, 'How much did natural talent play a part in achieving their level of success?'

In drawing on scientific research and real-life case studies, the book acknowledges that the old view was that genius was hereditary and what we could achieve in life was largely determined for us before we got here.

Francis Galton, who authored the book *Hereditary Genius* in 1869, coined the expression 'nature versus nurture'. Galton argued that people had innate limits in what they could achieve in life and, regardless of the work they put in, they would never break past these predetermined boundaries. It's best if they just accept that, stay within their boundaries and 'find true moral repose in an honest conviction that he is engaged in as much good work as his nature rendered him capable of performing'. In other words, give up and be content.

This explains a lot of the thought patterns in our culture that surround great performers and the notion that they operate at an unattainable standard. An idea that you either have it or you don't.

Over a hundred years passed and the research continued. Hundreds of studies have considered the same subject, such as the employees whose performance had plateaued for years, seemingly hitting their 'rigidly determinate natural limits', only to a see a consistent improvement in performance after new incentives were offered. Or the child who grew into a teenager, never showing any real promise until finding something they were truly engaged with.

In his now famous paper, 'The role of deliberate practice in the acquisition of expert performance', Swedish psychologist and the world's leading researcher on what builds expertise, Anders Ericsson, said that 'the search for stable heritable characteristics that could predict or at least account for superior performance ... has been surprisingly unsuccessful'. Meaning that, after countless case studies, researchers found no relationship between natural talent and great performance.

However, at the time this paper was written in 1993, 'natural talent' was still the favoured theory to explain high achievers. Ericsson indicated that 'the conviction in the importance of talent appears to be based on the insufficiency of alternative hypotheses'. Meaning people believe in 'talent' because they don't have any alternative explanation of high achievement.

Until now.

The new research outlined by psychologists such as Ericsson indicates that the number one determinant of an individual's success comes down to how many hours they spend on 'deliberate practice', which in our language means hard work combined with ongoing learning.

Mozart's father was a professional composer who, when Mozart was born, stopped composing music to dedicate his time to training Mozart on how to compose music. The myth that formed from generation to generation was that Mozart was a born genius, composing symphonies in his teenage years. While Mozart was playing and composing music in his teenage years, they were not his original works; he was simply borrowing music from composers and musicians he respected, and playing their music. He was always open and transparent about this, but as the tale travelled from generation to generation, the story changed to a more glorified one.

Tiger Woods was also born to a professional golfer who also studied the most effective strategies for training young golfers. Before Tiger could walk, his father would take him to the garage, sit him in his high chair and start to hit golf balls into a net in the garage. 'It was as if he was watching a movie,' Tiger's father has said. Both Tiger and his father have written books and not once have they attributed Tiger's success to natural talent; rather, the very deliberate practices he engages in every single day to transcend the ups and downs of golf.

The greats in any field, be it sport, science or business, are definitely on another level; the new science simply suggests that they were not born there.

Business, like anything else, is a skill, and how good you become at starting, building and managing great companies will come down to how hard you work and how much time and energy you spend in ongoing learning.

A business will never outgrow its founder. Your rate of learning as an entrepreneur will determine how far your brand will reach.

As Tiger Woods says about golf, 'It is the game for a lifetime.'

@jackdelosa
A business will never outgrow its founder.
#unprofessional

the entrepreneur's ladder

As in any field, in business there is a progression that great entrepreneurs go through in order to reach the top of their field.

It takes a unique person to start a business, and an even more special person to be able to grow that business into a multimillion-dollar company. The reason the creation of multimillion-dollar businesses is so rare is that, at every different stage, the game changes slightly and so the way an entrepreneur manages and leads the organisation needs to change too.

the ENTREPRENEUR'S ladder

$10m +	**SELL**	*Investor*
$5m - $10m	**STRATEGY**	*Chess Master*
$1m - $5m	**SCALE**	*Business Person*
$100k - $1m	**START-UP**	*Street-fighter*
$0 - $100k	**SEED**	*Explorer*
$0 - $100k	**STUDENT**	*Learner*

One of the biggest barriers to growth I see in business is that, as a business comes out of the start-up stage and starts to become a more established company, the founders still think and act in the same way they did through the start-up phase. This will place a permanent glass ceiling on the size and reach of the business, until the founders recognise that they are in fact overseeing a *different* organisation that requires very different leadership.

Let's look at the different stages of businesses (see table 1), the challenges you'll face each step of the way, what you can do to get to the next level and who you need to be at each different stage.

Table 1: the entrepreneur's ladder

Revenue	Stage of business	Description	You	Your approach	Critical success factor
$10m+	Sell	This is where you may look to continue sitting on the board; you may look at options to exit the business; or you might consider taking the company public. This stage is about maximising value and the time to start thinking about how and when you will extract some value.	Investor	As an investor you need to think about how you can maximise the value of what you have built. This might be through expanding into different markets, acquiring other businesses, taking the company public or exiting the business. This is about how you achieve the highest financial return for your investment.	Value
$5m–$10m	Strategy	In the strategy stage you have a larger business and it is time to start thinking about maximising the *value* of the business. This will involve putting an experienced management team in place and removing yourself from the business.	Chess master	In the strategy stage you have a larger base; no longer can you turn on a dime; no longer do you know every staff member by their first name. It is a larger organisation and therefore requires thorough planning, financial management and vision for the future.	Foresight
$1m–$5m	Scale	In the scale stage you have created a viable business model; now it is time to scale it. This is about identifying the best path for growth and what options are available to you for expansion. This should also be where you continue to dilute your operational involvement in the business.	Business person	If start-up is 95 per cent act and 5 per cent think, in scale stage the game changes and you should be diluting yourself out of the operations of the business. You want to get to a point where you have a great team within the business and your role becomes 5 per cent act and 95 per cent think.	Commercial intelligence

(continued)

Table 1: *(cont'd)*

Revenue	Stage of business	Description	You	Your approach	Critical success factor
$100k–$1m	Start-up	During the start-up phase you are a temporary organism designed to find a viable business model. This is where you need to have your product to market fit, your message to market fit and build a profitable model.	Street-fighter	We know people want to buy it — we now need to put a business around the product. This will involve working out the best marketing, sales, delivery, customer service and accounting principles to put in place to build a business. This will involve much trial and error and you have to be happy to fail forward. In the start-up phase you are a hustler; here it is 95 per cent act, 5 per cent think.	Resilience
$100k–$100k	Seed	In the seed stage you have identified what industry you want to go into and developed a business idea; now it is time to test the idea by launching in the leanest possible way, and to learn lessons as quickly and inexpensively as possible.	Explorer	This is the stage where you want to test your product or service quickly, spending as little money as possible. Don't build your perfect website yet or enter into a lease for shop or office space; simply put your product or service out into the market-place to see if people want to buy it.	Resourcefulness
$0–$100k	Student	You don't have a business yet, but rather you are studying the game of business in a broad sense.	Learner	You need to learn as much as you can about business through researching, reading books, speaking with people and attending educational events. Here you want to find a marriage between what you love and a strong business opportunity.	Rate of learning

Chapter 1

VISION

When Steve Jobs was forced out of Apple in 1985, he founded a company called NeXT, ensuring that he and all his team wore hoodies with just two words printed on them: 'We're NeXT!'

In a 1985 interview, an interviewer points out that Jobs does not have a corporate background; he is not an engineer; he is not a manufacturer; he is not a distributor; nor is he a retailer. The interviewer asks that if Steve is none of these things, then what does he personally do? He responds:

> There needs to be someone who is the keeper and the reiterater of the vision. Because there's just a ton of work to do and when you have to walk a thousand miles and you take the first step it looks like a long way and it really helps if there's someone there saying 'we're one step closer, the goal definitely exists, it's not just a mirage out there.' So in a thousand and one little, and sometimes larger ways, the vision needs to be reiterated. I do that a lot.

As entrepreneurs we spend our lives tinkering with a universe that doesn't yet exist. We are creating a world, a business, a model, a product, a team that today doesn't exist, but tomorrow will hopefully be great.

Too often it's too easy to dismiss any sight into the future as 'guessing' or 'dreaming', yet as an entrepreneur this is your job, first and foremost. People look to you for direction—your staff, your partners, your customers, your suppliers, the media. When you put your hand up as the leader of a company, your very first job—and it's a job that never ends—is to create the compelling vision that inspires people to push that vision forward.

This means knowing what you want the business to be 10 years from now, and knowing your top three objectives for the coming 12 months, while managing monthly targets to ensure that these objectives are met.

In 1996, just over 10 years after establishing the company, Jobs ended up selling NeXT to Apple for $429 million, plus stock, and once again became the CEO of the company he had founded in his parents' garage.

@jackdelosa
The entrepreneur that wins is the entrepreneur that can best create the universe that doesn't yet exist. #uprofessional

know your why

When I was eight years old my parents ran a not-for-profit organisation called Breaking the Cycle. Breaking the Cycle would take long-term unemployed youth off the streets, put them through a three-month training program and then help them find work.

Breaking the Cycle was one of the most successful job placement agencies for long-term unemployed youth in Australia, and so a large amount of their funding came from the federal government and Commonwealth Employment Services, an organisation the government had set up to manage unemployment benefits. Although they were a not-for-profit organisation, they turned over millions of dollars each year and changed the lives of thousands of kids, some of whom lived with my family and me.

SEE

THINGS

INVISIBLE

Seeing how so many young people were brought up and how the traditional system didn't cater to or support these kids made me realise at a very young age that there were more important things in the world than what I was supposed to be learning at school.

In 1995, when the federal government shut down the Commonwealth Employment Services, Breaking the Cycle was unsuccessful in finding funding elsewhere. The organisation collapsed and the hundreds of kids they saw every year were now without the kind of support they needed to lead purposeful lives.

This sent a very loud message to me at a young age: that the world does need people who can change things, although to do this also requires business smarts and a commercial nous that sees these types of social enterprises run in a sustainable and meaningful way. In my father's words, 'You can't just rely on love, trust and pixie dust.'

This is why I do what I do. Business for me has never been about the money or the 'stuff'. It is about gaining financial integrity, a reputation and a team of great people who can make a lasting difference to the way people live their lives.

Having a strong 'why' means that, when things get hard, which they often do, I can see past the challenges and keep moving forward.

Why are you in business? Why are you so intent on facing and conquering this challenge?

Discover this and remind yourself of it every day.

eyes wide shut

Too often when creating a compelling vision for our life or our business, we look at what already exists. We create a vision with our eyes wide open, pulling ideas from what has already been created in the hope that we can improve it slightly.

This works, and it is safe.

A more radical way to form a vision for your life and your business is to do so with your eyes wide shut. Meaning, if you were to draw ideas and inspiration from within, rather than from without, what would you see?

In a speech in Dublin, Ireland, in 1963, John F. Kennedy, then president of the United States, said 'We need people who can dream of things that never were.'

Too often we discount the voice inside our head, believing the opinions of others to be more credible than our own. But entrepreneurship is about giving life and volume to the voice inside your head and following your own path, not one that has been laid out by someone else.

When the voice inside your head is louder than the voices outside of your head, you have begun to master your life.

the bigger the vision, the easier it is to execute

Counterintuitively, often in business the larger the vision, the easier it is to execute. When you have a compelling vision, grounded in substance and communicated with confidence, people and resources follow.

Too often we can be misled into believing that if we aim small we are more likely to achieve our outcome, but in my experience the opposite has proven to be true. When you paint an eyes wide shut vision that truly speaks to the hearts and minds of the people you want to inspire, people will feel that this is a vision worth being a part of.

A strong vision not only sticks with people, but also becomes remarkable—meaning people will remark upon it. Provided the vision is credible and the right team is in place to implement it, people will amplify your vision everywhere they go.

It is often said that most people are silently begging to be led. Painting an audacious and ambitious vision that exceeds what people are familiar with inspires people to want to be a part of what you're setting out to do. As an entrepreneur, you need to be comfortable leading other business leaders, executives, investors and the media. To lead the leaders and do this with charisma is what great entrepreneurs do best.

12-month road map

Grand visions need to be translated into concise plans. As a small- to medium-sized business, the way we plan and communicate our plans needs to be vastly different to how it's done in a corporation or how it's taught at university.

@jackdelosa
Grand visions need to translate into concise plans. #unprofessional

In an early-stage or growth-stage business, people need direction, clarity and inspiration quickly. Whether we're communicating with employees, potential partners, investors or other stakeholders we should always be selling the future—acknowledging where we are today and emphasising where we plan to be in the future.

Go to www.unprofessional.com.au/bonuses to download your editable version of the 12-month road map.

12 MONTH
road map

TOP 3 OBJECTIVES

1 ....
2 ....
3 ....

QUARTERLY OBJECTIVES

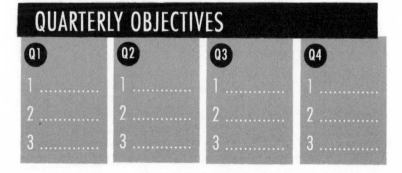

Q1

1 ....
2 ....
3 ....

Q2

1 ....
2 ....
3 ....

Q3

1 ....
2 ....
3 ....

Q4

1 ....
2 ....
3 ....

For that reason, your 12-month road map needs to be simple and brief. It needs to fit on one page. It was Sir Richard Branson, founder of the Virgin Group, who said, 'Any fool can make something complicated. It is hard to make something simple.' In summarising and communicating our plans we need to fight for brevity and fight for simplicity.

TIP

A good 12-month road map will include:

➤ the three core objectives you will achieve in the 12-month period

➤ three quarterly objectives for each quarter of the year.

Your vision will only ever be as strong as your plan and the team you put behind it. It is imperative that, as the leader of your business, you give everyone around you crystal clear clarity about the direction and objectives of the business, both long term with the vision and short term with the road map.

Fill in your 12-month road map and make copies of it so it is visible to you and your team at all times. This helps everyone not get distracted with projects that are not core and to stay focused on what truly matters.

Chapter 2

START BEFORE YOU'RE READY

There is never a good time to start a business. The stars will never align. You will never have enough time, money or information to start a business. A job opportunity, a promotion, moving house, not knowing where to start, no experience, no mentors, no savings, no idea, too young, too old, too clever, too dumb, too in love, too comfortable ... These are just some of the dream killers that prevent people from starting to build great things.

Great entrepreneurs start before they're ready. While others are planning, researching or waiting, real entrepreneurs get going.

Being in business for yourself brings a lot of uncertainty. Uncertainty around money, around timelines, around whether you will ultimately succeed or fail. As a business owner you need to train yourself, one step at a time, to become comfortable with being uncomfortable. This won't happen overnight, but as you start with one small step and start to carry a little bit of uncertainty in your life, that risk will slowly build to a point where, a couple of years down the track, you will be taking calculated risks every day that would make any other person nervous.

When I was 18 I was studying for a commerce–law degree in Melbourne. I had a great job, was enrolled in a good course and had a support network that was cheering me on every step of the way.

I threw it all in.

Inspired by looking at business people who had gone before me, one day as I walked into class, I sat down, said goodbye to my friends and walked out, never to return.

After being rejected by four different lenders, I was finally able to borrow $20 000 from a very reluctant bank and buy into my first start-up, a business-to-business call centre that I would start with two people slightly older than me. In a matter of weeks I had gone from a cushy job that paid well, studying for a good degree with great career prospects and being cheered on by everyone around me to being part of a start-up business (otherwise known as being unemployed), $20 000 in debt, with zero income and a very concerned and discouraging group of friends and family.

I loved it. Finally I was in the game. Finally I had taken the step and was in the arena.

Having studied so many successful entrepreneurs before then, I was well aware that it was very likely this business wasn't going to succeed. I was okay with that: I viewed it as my apprenticeship. Rather than spending $40 000 and five years 'learning' at uni, I would spend $20 000 and a few years learning about business in the real world. I thought, hey, who knows, maybe it will work out.

It didn't. We started losing money, going backwards, working harder than anyone else we knew while not taking home even a wage, let alone a profit. We had spread ourselves too thin, tried to do too many things, and so the bills, wages, tax payments were all piling up, and, as a start-up business, we simply didn't have the cash flow to support it. We dug ourselves a financial hole so deep that at different times my business partners had to take time out due to the stress and pressure of the situation.

However, after making some fundamental changes to our business model and leadership team, we began to climb out of trouble inch by inch, step by step. After another 18 months we saw the light of day; we were no longer in debt, and had pulled ourselves up out of trouble.

Although this was a very stressful and even discouraging introduction to business, I knew that almost every successful entrepreneur I had ever looked at had found themselves in a similar situation and often hadn't got out of it unscathed as I was.

I loved it. Not in the moment; in the moment I hated it. It was Muhammad Ali who said, 'I hated every minute of training, but I said, "Don't quit. Suffer now and live the rest of your life as a champion."' As entrepreneurs we don't hate 'every minute' of it, but we do recognise that, particularly during the start-up phase of business, we will be challenged more than we have ever been challenged before. Like a marathon runner who learns to love the strain of training, business owners must learn to love the pressures that come hand in hand with being the master of your own destiny.

Today I am onto my fourth business. Two of those businesses are now multimillion-dollar enterprises—MBE Education, which helps small- and medium-sized enterprises raise money from investors and sell their business, and The Entourage, which from nothing has grown into Australia's largest educator of entrepreneurs under 40. MBE Education has helped our clients collectively execute hundreds of millions of dollars in investment transactions, while The Entourage is today an army of over 35000 young entrepreneurs from the start-up phase right through to businesses doing revenues of $20 million each year.

I continue to work incredibly hard and challenge myself every single day, only these days I am a lot more comfortable financially. When I was 23, due to the success of MBE Education, I was in a position where I could buy my mum's house to help her retire, which made the incredibly difficult early days seem worthwhile. I'm fortunate enough to be able to take my entire team on overseas holidays to stay in luxurious holiday destinations, help my father with his investments and personally invest into early-stage companies that are led by highly successful entrepreneurs.

I'm in a position where I'm regularly meeting and working with some of the smartest minds in the world, regularly being called on by media, and launching not-for-profit projects such as The Entourage Foundation to deliver business education in high schools throughout Australia.

I have achieved all of this because I wasn't afraid to start and fail my way forward. Today the people that told me I was crazy for even trying are the ones who now tell me I'm lucky.

Start.

stay lean

In the beginning of any new business or any new project, do not invest heavily in anything or anyone before you have proven that the product or service you are going to provide is what the customer wants. Often new businesses (or even existing businesses) launching new projects will invest in a fully functional, perfectly designed website, an accountant, business cards, stock, maybe even some office space, and spend months and months building a product or service. After spending tens of thousands of dollars and six months building something, they finally take their idea to market and try to sell it.

The flaw in this approach is that we are investing all that time, effort and money building something that is based on our own assumptions—which, if you're anything like me, are often incorrect. Worse, we have done all of this without any input from the very person we're doing it all for: the customer.

Instead, any early-stage business needs to get to market as quickly and as cheaply as possible, and test their product, business model and marketing in the real world to find out whether there is a demand for this product or service.

This might include setting up a basic website, encouraging people to simply 'opt in' to join your mailing list and tracking the percentage of visitors that do. It might also be launching a Facebook group and assessing its popularity, and even engaging in conversations within the group to get firsthand insight from people who are in your target market. Or you could develop an inexpensive prototype and try to sell a few before investing heavily in creating the real deal.

Once you have had enough feedback from real people about the popularity and saleability of what you're doing and the concept is relatively proven, you will then have more confidence and insight before you invest more time and perhaps money into the business. Best-case scenario is that the initial sales you make will essentially finance the development of the rest of the business.

When you start out in business there are hundreds of lessons to learn between the starting point and the point of profitability. Learn these lessons as quickly and as cheaply as possible. Once you have found a profitable model, scale it.

fail fast

Our culture tells us that failure is a bad thing: we should try to avoid making mistakes; if we get the answer wrong we'll fail the test. As a business owner, however, you need to embrace failure. You need to welcome it and become its friend. You need to be okay with the fact that you will probably make the 'wrong' decision *most* of the time. This is how entrepreneurs learn; there is no textbook you can follow.

My measure of success for any start-up business is not necessarily how much money you make, but rather how quickly you can learn. Learning doesn't happen in the writing of a perfectly designed business plan; learning happens when you step foot into the arena and launch your business, however unprepared you may think you are, and begin to fail forward.

@jackdelosa
Learning doesn't happen in the writing of a perfectly designed business plan. Fail forward. #unprofessional

A start-up business is simply a temporary organism designed to find a viable business model. When you are in the start-up phase of business you are a teenager who doesn't know what you want to be when you grow up. You want to grow up—you probably want to grow up in a hurry—you just don't know what you're going to look like when you do.

The only way we can find a profitable business model is through what's called iteration. Launch something (a product, a marketing campaign, a new project), figure out what doesn't work, bring it back in, change. Launch again, figure out what doesn't work, bring it back in, change. Launch again, figure out what doesn't work, bring it back in, change. This is the job of any early-stage business—to make decisions, implement quickly, monitor the success or otherwise of the project and make improvements rapidly. Iterate.

This is our advantage. While larger organisations are having meetings about having meetings, drafting up strategy documents, getting sign off from several layers of management, running it through their legal team, we, as early-stage businesses, are moving. We are in the arena, engaged with the consumer, working out what they want and what they don't want, and figuring out a better way of achieving development and delivery.

John Ilhan, founder of Crazy John's and number one on the inaugural BRW Young Rich List in 2002 with a personal net worth of $200 million (rising to $300 million the next year), said, 'If you want to become successful twice as fast, double the amount of mistakes you're making.' As a business owner you will make more 'mistakes' in a week than most people do in a year: this is required if you are to truly succeed.

a hungry crowd

If you were starting a restaurant, what's the number one thing you would want in order to ensure the success of the restaurant? Great food, great people, a nice menu, a good location?

I would argue that the number one thing you want as a new restaurant is a hungry crowd. If you can find a group of people who are actually searching for what you have to offer, the battle is half won.

Often we see people launching products that are great in theory, but don't actually solve any real problem. Do not become a solution looking for a problem. Everything that you build as an entrepreneur must directly solve a problem for your target audience. At the very least if it doesn't solve a real problem, it needs to make their life better.

Part of staying lean is about searching for your hungry crowd without spending too much time or money in the meantime. Once you have identified a gap in the market, and a real problem that you can solve, that's when the fun starts.

A little over a year ago, Lorraine Murphy, a member of The Entourage Scalable and Saleable Program, identified that big brands, such as Woolworths and L'Oréal, wanted to reach more mums online. Having been in PR and media for nine years, Lorraine was familiar with the landscape and saw an opportunity for these brands to start engaging with 'mummy bloggers'. Mummy bloggers, who are becoming increasingly popular, are writers who have audiences of hundreds of thousands of mums online, and through their blogs write about how to make life easier for mums.

After talking to some large household brands to ensure this was a real need, Lorraine rallied together a panel of mummy bloggers and started selling them into large brands as a genuine advertising channel for these brands to reach more mums.

Lorraine identified a genuine problem, in that these household brands wanted to reach mums in a more direct and meaningful way, and also discovered that mummy bloggers wanted help in partnering with these brands so that they could earn an income doing what they loved.

Lorraine had found her hungry crowd.

Immediately launching her new company the Remarkables Group, out of the spare bedroom in her apartment, Lorraine signed brands such as Coles, Woolworths, L'Oréal, Commonwealth Bank, AMEX, ING, Nivea, Schwarzkopf, Johnson & Johnson, BlackBerry, EA, Nutella, Moccona and SunRice. Lorraine hit $1.1 million revenue in her first 12 months of operation and is now looking at the UK and the US for further expansion.

know your customer

Sam Prince is a young entrepreneur who has achieved more than most will in a lifetime. He founded Zambrero, a fresh Mexican chain of restaurants with 28 stores. It has been listed as *BRW*'s Fastest Growing Franchise in Australia by Store Numbers in 2011. Sam started Zambrero when he was studying full time to become a doctor. He has since founded One Disease at a Time, a not-for-profit foundation set up to eradicate one disease at a time from Australia (he did become a doctor), started a high-end Mexican restaurant chain called Mejico and is also building a business that focuses on stem-cell research and development.

Having a cocktail or two with me in Double Bay one Saturday night (Sam rocked up wearing a Zambrero t-shirt), Sam looked at me with the sort of intensity only Sam can and said, 'Jack, when it comes to business I believe in one God: Customer.' What Sam was saying is that in any business how well you understand your customer, and therefore how well you serve your customer, will determine the success of the business.

As a business owner you must obsess about your customer. You need to get to know them better than they know themselves. Why they buy from you, where they get their information from, where they hang out on the weekends, who their friends are, how often they buy from you, why they prefer you or your product over your competitors, what their dreams are, what they fear, who they see themselves as, who they aspire to be.

This depth of true understanding may take years to develop, but it is an understanding that will stand you apart from the rest of the crowd who are standing in their shop or sitting at their desk wondering why the phone doesn't ring.

UNPROFESSIONAL CUSTOMER PROFILING QUESTIONS

Through speaking with your target market, either face to face, over the phone or through surveys, find answers to questions like:

➤ Is X a problem for you?

➤ Why is X a problem for you?

➤ Where do you currently go to solve this problem?

➤ What is great about this solution?

➤ How could this solution be improved?

➤ Where do you currently find information about the solution (magazines, websites, associations, ads)?

➤ What would the ideal product or service do that solves this problem?

➤ What characteristics would you look for in a brand that solved this problem?

➤ What would solving this problem mean for you?

➤ How would you best like to access the product or service that would solve this problem?

---

know your market

At a micro level you need to understand your customer; at a macro level you need to understand your market.

One of the common mistakes people make when starting a business is to think that their market is 'everybody' or 'everybody over 30'. The clearer and more specific you can be about exactly the kind of person you are trying to reach, the better you will be able to communicate with that person and the better you will be able to deliver value to that person. When we try to be everything to everyone we end up being nothing to anyone. Identify with great specificity the exact person you are targeting.

Once you know the profile of your customer, you then need to ask whether the market is big enough to build a business for. Is this a business that can grow to be a significant size or, due to the limitations of the market, will it be a 'lifestyle business' that can generate some good cash flow, but may not build into a multimillion-dollar company?

In knowing your market you want to look at the size of the market, the likelihood of the market paying for what you're offering, the competitors and similar businesses in the same space, and the business models that have worked or failed in this market. Identify whether there are any larger businesses that are acquiring businesses in this industry that you could one day sell to—more on this chapter 8, 'Play the bigger game'.

As a business owner you have two best friends: Google and mentors. You can find the information you are looking for, first by researching on Google and second by speaking with people who have experience in that industry or a similar industry.

It is important you know the lay of the land so you can strategise where you fit in that marketplace and, paradoxically, how you can stand out.

be the dumbest person in the room

It is my aim to be the dumbest person in the room at all times. As an entrepreneur you need to surround yourself with people who are smarter than you.

@jackdelosa
It is my aim to be the dumbest person in the room at all times. #unprofessional

This does not take the place of your own learning and your own intelligence; however, the greats of business have achieved what they have because they are comfortable in admitting they don't have all the answers.

An old business partner and close friend of mine, Reuben Buchanan, is the founder of *Wealth Creator* magazine. Reuben and I built a company called MBE Education together. During his *Wealth Creator* days Reuben asked Gerry Harvey, the founder of Harvey Norman, how he managed to achieve so much in his life and Harvey replied, 'I hire people who are smarter than me.' When Reuben questioned who was smarter than Gerry Harvey, who is a self-made Australian billionaire, Harvey replied:

> Not smarter in entrepreneurship, but my Operations Manager is better with operations than I am. My Financial Controller knows more about financial management than I do. When I want to do something new in business I ask myself who is the best in the world at that and I take them to lunch.

As an early-stage business owner, surrounding yourself with people who are smarter than you means finding and building relationships with people who know more about business than you do, and taking them to coffee once a month. One of the things that surprised me when I first went into business was how willing highly successful people were to help me.

Every successful entrepreneur got to where they are with the help of some amazing people. In the early days of their career the people who helped them weren't their employees or directors, but other successful entrepreneurs who said 'yes' to having coffee. Building a business is not easy—in fact it's one of the hardest things you can choose to do—and people with experience know this. Send them a message over LinkedIn, send them a letter, give them a call, subscribe to their mailing list.

In 2010 I set up The Entourage, which is now Australia's largest community of entrepreneurs under 40, as a way to create a place where entrepreneurs can come to connect with like-minded people and receive real-world education and advice from some of the best entrepreneurs in the world. The success stories that continually come out of young entrepreneurs in The Entourage are a testament to what can happen when we get out of our own way and surround ourselves with the right people.

You will never find a treasure map and fortunately there is no rule book for becoming an entrepreneur; however the next best thing is to find people with 'been there, done that' experience and ask the hard questions.

the three rules of start-up

As a start-up business it is so tempting to spread ourselves too thinly across too many projects, too many products and even perhaps too many businesses.

We look at Richard Branson overseeing 400 companies, with a net worth of $8 billion, from his iPhone while lying on a hammock on Necker Island and think to ourselves, 'Yeah, I could do that.'

What a lot of people don't realise is that Branson started his first successful business, Virgin Records, in 1971, after a string of failures. It wasn't until 1981 when Virgin Records was highly profitable that he opened another business, Virgin Games. In 1992, 21 years after he had started the company, Branson sold Virgin Records to EMI for $1 billion. He decided to go ahead with this sale in order to save another one of his companies, Virgin Atlantic, from the brink of collapse.

More recently, Branson, through Virgin Unite, set up a string of not-for-profit business schools for young people in developing nations. A friend of mine, Creel Price, who sold his business for $109 million in 2008, and I were engaged to develop the curriculum for the Branson Centre of Entrepreneurship in South Africa. After flying to Johannesburg to meet the students, the full-time mentors and Branson himself, Creel and I spent 10 days working with the school and the students to familiarise ourselves with the culture and what these kids needed in order to become better business people.

On the last day of our visit the students had set up booths to demonstrate their businesses to the mentors and to Branson. One of the young students that I had become good friends with, Cleopatra Simelane, showed Branson her magazine, called *Student Magazine*. When she told him about the reach the magazine had in schools throughout South Africa, he looked at the advertisers she had in the magazine, noticing she had ads from top-tier brands—advertising that she had built from nothing. Branson, visibly impressed by what Cleo had achieved in just a few short years, reflected, 'It's so important as a growing magazine to simply focus on selling advertising; you've obviously managed to do just that.'

Having started a magazine of his own in 1968, also called *Student Magazine*, which didn't succeed, I suspect Branson was talking from experience.

Often people ask me what's the number one thing that prevents start-up businesses from succeeding. My answer is simple: 'They don't focus.' The biggest and most common mistake start-up businesses make is that they simply try to do too many things and, in doing so, do nothing particularly well. Often the hardest thing for any entrepreneurially minded person is to say 'no' to opportunities and just focus on core business. Once your core business, whatever that may be, is highly profitable, you can then start to look at other markets, other products and other growth opportunities.

I once did an on-camera interview with Siimon Reynolds in the back of a black Mercedes as we drove to Sydney Airport. Siimon co-founded Photon Group, a group of advertising and marketing companies, which at its peak reached a valuation of $500 million. When I asked Siimon what he thought start-up businesses needed to do in order to succeed, his answer was simple yet difficult: 'Pick one thing and become the best in the world at it.'

Stick to the three rules of start-up: Focus. Focus. Focus.

Chapter 3

BUILD AN ATTRACTION MODEL

When we are building an early-stage business, we have less. We have less than our competitors and less than the businesses we're aiming to disrupt. Less people, less money, less track record, less insight, less customers and perhaps even less credibility. But we need to do more with less.

In the movie *Moneyball*, starring Brad Pitt, the Oakland A's, a major league baseball team, are confronted with the fact that, while the New York Yankees have a budget of $125 million for player recruitment, the Oakland A's have a budget of just $41 million. The main character, club manager Billy Beane (Brad Pitt), has to find a way to compete with the rest of the field, even though they have significantly less money. Beane must innovate.

In a telling scene, Beane is having a meeting with his player selection committee, a table of older, more experienced baseball professionals who are clinging to the way things have always been done and putting forward the same status-quo suggestions that got the Oakland A's into this position. Beane, visibly frustrated, insists to his older counterparts that they 'must think differently' if they are to be competitive in a fight where they are significantly disadvantaged. In a line that has become a catch phrase throughout my businesses,

Beane profoundly states, 'If we play like the Yankees in here, we will lose to the Yankees out there.'

Small businesses are not smaller versions of big businesses. Small business is a completely different ball game. How we advertise, build our brand and attract customers needs to be vastly different from the way big businesses behave.

While larger businesses can *push* out marketing messages with budgets of millions of dollars, early-stage businesses need to find a way to *attract* customers to come to them. To build an attraction model is to put yourself where opportunity can see you and customers can find you without your having to pay for it. This is the skill of an entrepreneur.

As early-stage businesses, we need to become masters of leverage—the art of doing more with less. We need to establish partnerships with complementary businesses that give us access to thousands, maybe even hundreds of thousands, of targeted prospective customers for free. We need to understand how to get noticed in the media so that we can build our brand with zero budget using public relations (PR) in ways that cut through the advertising our larger competitors pay for. Rather than paying to advertise through channels like television and newspapers, we need to build our own database of contacts and build our own community so that we can create genuine and direct relationships with our target market, rather than talking at them through overly produced ads that we can't afford even if we wanted to use them.

These are the strategies we'll be talking about in this chapter.

In *Moneyball*, after developing an innovative and remarkably different way of identifying and recruiting players who are undervalued, Billy Beane's Oakland A's go on to win 20 games in a row in the season of 2002, setting the American League record. The movie is based on a true story.

BUILD AN *attraction* · MODEL ·

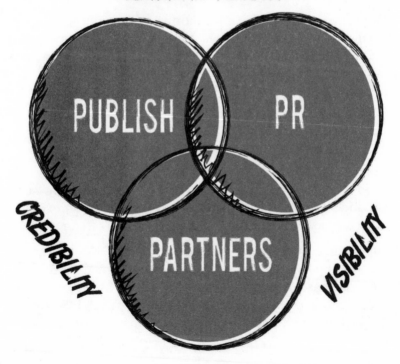

REMARK-ABILITY

PUBLISH

PR

PARTNERS

CREDIBILITY

VISIBILITY

strategic partnerships

Size matters. Yet most business owners have an ineffective strategy for getting big. Approaching a growth strategy on your own, without leveraging through large organisations, is one of the quickest ways to ensure you remain small.

When I reflect on the businesses I have had that didn't go well, and the businesses I've started since, which have gone well, the main difference is that with the businesses that did well, we adopted a leveraged approach to finding new customers.

Rather than cold calling, trying to set up meetings with companies that didn't know us or spending money on sterile advertising, I started to build strategic partnerships with complementary businesses that would allow us to leverage their customer base and reach a targeted prospect.

When we started MBE Education—a company that helps small to medium businesses raise money from investors, and buy and sell businesses—we had ambitious growth targets that simply weren't going to be achieved if we adopted the same old approach.

Instead, we created a strategic partnership with another business that had a list of 120000 business owners, who were all interested in growing and expanding their business, but had never been taught how to raise money, or buy or sell a business. Our new partner was itself also looking for new products and services that would add value to its existing database so they could broaden their service offering.

After three meetings with this company, we set up a partnership whereby they would market our services to their database of 120000 business owners who were actively looking to expand, and we would give them a percentage of the revenue we earned from any clients that came from them.

What this enabled us to do was reach 120000 highly targeted prospects in a way that wasn't pushy or needed cold calling, but rather worked through a referral from a company they already had a relationship with and trusted. And all of this with zero dollars' outlay and three meetings.

Twelve months later, in 2009, MBE Education was listed in the Fastest 50 Growing Start-Ups in Australia by SmartCompany, one of Australia's leading online business publications, as a result of the rapid growth we had achieved off the back of a successful strategic partnership strategy.

A strategic partnership is simply a win-win relationship between two complementary businesses.

@jackdelosa
A strategic partnership is a win-win relationship between two complementary businesses. #unprofessional

In an early-stage business, if you can develop some consistent partnerships with complementary businesses that continually drive new customers to you, then you have put yourself in a very leveraged position where *customers will find you*. This is one aspect of building an attraction model.

the three steps to setting up a strategic partnership

Strategic partnerships are the most effective and fastest way for any start-up or early-stage business to win customers and accelerate growth on a shoestring budget. Let's explore the three things you need to do in order to set these up for your business:

1 Find a complementary business.

2 Develop a compelling reason for the partnership.

3 Develop a compelling offer.

find a complementary business

The first step to creating a successful strategic partnership is to find a complementary business. A complementary business is one that you can add value to in some way, and they can drive you business from their existing customer list. While most partners will be interested in looking at how you can help them monetise their existing audience or how you can help drive them new customers, in the start-up phase, before you have built your own audience, this can be difficult. It's very important to get creative and first determine what value you can offer another organisation, before we start to chat to them about creating a partnership — there's more discussion of this below in the section 'develop a compelling reason'.

Regardless of how you're delivering value to a partner, the value they need to be delivering to you is to help you reach a qualified customer list in order to generate new business for you.

In order to identify a complementary business, ask yourself three questions:

- Where do my customers go before they come to me?
- Where do my customers go after they buy my product?
- Who targets the same market that I do, but offers a different product or service?

where do my customers go before they come to me?

At MBE Education we knew, because we understood our clients very well, that the first place a business owner goes when they want to raise money is their accountant; however, most of the time the accountant doesn't know how to assist the business in raising the capital. This makes accountants a great partner for MBE because they have a trusted relationship with their clients; they are actively being asked if they can help the client to raise money;

and MBE Education is not seen to be competing with the accountant, because we are not accountants.

If you are a personal trainer your customers might be signing up at a gym or consulting a nutrition specialist before they search for a personal trainer.

If you are an online fashion store, your customers might first be visiting an online jewellery store.

If you are an electrician, they might first call a carpenter or plumber.

If you are a web-developer, your customers might first call a web designer or brand strategist.

Identify where your customers go before they come to you and this will be a rich source of potential win-win partnerships.

where do my customers go after they buy my product?

Where your customers go *after* they buy your product is also a good channel to explore in order to find more qualified partnerships.

When working with a car brokerage that wanted to create a steady flow of customers coming to the business, we explored where their customers were going after they decided they wanted to buy a car. Through discussions we found that the car brokerage was sending all of its customers who wanted finance to a particular financier, who helped these people borrow the money they required in order to purchase a car. While this was already a value-add for the car brokerage, we felt there was more opportunity to be explored to make this arrangement even more fruitful for both parties.

In approaching the company, we struck a deal to formalise the arrangement to make this finance company the exclusive financier for all cars that were bought through the business. In exchange, the car brokerage would include the finance company in their monthly newsletter, which went out to their database of 17 000 every month. This meant more visibility for the car brokerage directly to people who were able to access finance, and an exclusive arrangement for the finance company to have a steady flow of customers coming their way.

The best strategic partnerships are formed with businesses that you have a logical tie to; if you have an existing relationship then this makes it even easier.

Where do your customers go after they come to you and how could you chat to these businesses about setting up a win-win partnership?

who targets the same market I do, but offers a different product or service?

Peter Moriarty, founder of itGenius and a Scalable and Saleable Member identified that, in order to grow, his IT support company needed to get in front of more targeted prospects in a leveraged way. Upon reflecting on one of the many partnerships he formed, Peter said:

> I identified an opportunity to form a strategic partnership with a non-competing business in a different industry to ours. They are an education organisation, we are technology consultants and we had a piece of technology that we could implement to improve the value participants received in their training programs.

Through identifying this one potential partnership and following the steps to create a strategic partnership, Peter created a deal that will deliver an immediate profit uplift for itGenius while delivering significant value to the end-user and the partner organisation.

> We negotiated a suitable price-point for the solution, which we agreed to split revenue 50/50 when taking it to market and we project our first-year revenue from the deal to exceed $250 000 in new business.

Here we have two completely different businesses—one is in technology consulting and the other in education—but the two companies share one thing: they have the same customer.

Ask yourself, who else services your target market and how could you work together?

In identifying answers to each of the three questions above, you will start to build a 'target list' of potential partners for you and your organisation. Once you know who you want to target, you then need to work out what you're going to offer.

develop a compelling reason

It is very important that, when approaching potential partners, you lead with what you can give. It is imperative you ask yourself, 'What value can I deliver to this organisation?' and lead with that. In your initial communication, what you want out of the partnership should be secondary.

> @jackdelosa
> **In business, always lead with what you can give.** #unprofessional

Your compelling reason might be that you have a list or a captive audience that you could promote the partner organisation to—you can do this even if you don't yet have the audience, but can demonstrate a growth path that shows that one day you will. You may be able to give a prospective partner sponsorship or advertising over some events or your website. Perhaps, by promoting your products and services, they can further add value to and monetise their existing audience by having a revenue or profit split for the customers they refer to your business. It might even be that you could create something especially for their audience that you can give away for free or at such a reduced rate that it comes as a gift to the strategic partner's customer.

If you are partnering with large corporates, they won't be interested in revenue or profit shares, but will be interested in two things: first, reaching an audience they can't otherwise reach; and second, helping them look good to their existing clientele.

For the first, if you have a database and a relationship with a certain niche in the market, chances are your relationship with that market segment has greater depth than the relationship the prospective partner has. Larger businesses are always trying to find ways of building better relationships with consumers, and going through smaller businesses is one way for them to do this.

For the second, helping them look good to their existing clients, you can provide a corporate with something that their customers will value so highly that the corporate will want to distribute it to their customers. This might be a research report, e-book, video series, special promotion or an exclusive product offering at a heavily reduced price.

If you're aiming to partner with small- to medium-sized businesses, they will also be interested in two things: first, a revenue or profit share; and second, cross-pollination.

Under the first model, both businesses track how many customers come to each of them from the strategic partner, and each party gives the partner a revenue or profit share from the customers they refer.

In cross-pollination, the question is, if they are referring you business and helping you find new clients, how can you do the same? In this instance you could market the partner to your customer list; advertise for them on your website; ask them to contribute to your blog; or give them sponsorship of certain events you are holding. Anything that helps them reach more targeted prospects.

> **TIP**
>
> Get creative about what you can do for your prospective partner, and make sure that you lead with this.

develop a compelling offer

Once you have identified a complementary business and developed a compelling reason for them to partner with you, you need to create a compelling offer that will go out to their customers. This is the offer that the partner will email to its database, send out through the post, advertise on its website or promote in whichever way you have agreed.

I have had a strategic partner send out an offer via email to a database of 70 000 and we got an uptake of seven people, which is an incredibly disappointing result from a reach that great. A month later that same partner sent another email to the same 70 000 and we had an uptake of 1600 people. The difference? The offer that went out in the second email was not selling something: instead, it offered a compelling lead magnet that was relevant to that audience — we had found our compelling offer.

The world has moved on from 'interruption marketing', which is 'stop, listen to me, buy from me'. We are now in an era of relationship marketing where brands need to create a relationship with prospective customers, often *before* the consumer is ready to purchase. The biggest mistake large businesses are still making today is that they are trying to sell something on the first touch point. Effective small businesses are now steering away from this approach. Disruptive start-ups realise that, in order to engage a prospective customer, we must offer something of value at the first contact, build a relationship and then discuss doing business together down the track.

In today's business world people build influence by producing and distributing great content. Not just giving people more information—more information is the last thing we need. But rather providing leadership and giving people step-by-step guidance for how to solve their current problems through educating them with effective lead magnets.

@jackdelosa
In today's business world you build influence by producing and distributing great content. #unprofessional

The most effective way to build a relationship with your target market is to educate them on the solution that they're coming to you for. This does not mean to educate them on your business, but to educate them on the solution that they're looking for. In doing so you will build trust between them and your business.

If you are a personal trainer, you could develop reports, e-books or a video series about how to attain the level of health and vitality your prospects are searching for.

If you are a mortgage broker, you could produce a monthly market report to give people the latest updates on interest rates and new products on the market.

If you are an accountant, you could educate your target market on what they need to do in order to manage their finances better and minimise tax and you could do this through releasing reports, fact sheets, checklists, blog posts or videos. These would be your 'lead magnets'—assets you release into the marketplace in order to engage your audience before you ask them to buy from you.

Remember, regardless of the business you are in, today you are in the business of education. How can you better educate your audience on what they need to know, before they buy from you?

@jackdelosa
Regardless of what business you are in, today you are in the business of education.
#unprofessional

In order to identify what your target market needs to know, ask yourself one question: 'What are six to eight things my target market needs to know about the solution they're seeking?'

If you're not yet clear on what your customers need to know, simply find people who belong to your target market and ask them, 'What are your biggest challenges when it comes to [insert your solution here]?'

Here are some examples:

- What are your biggest challenges when it comes to raising money from investors?
- What are your biggest challenges when it comes to achieving health and fitness?
- What are your biggest challenges when it comes to managing your finances and minimising tax?
- What are your biggest challenges when it comes to purchasing good quality clothes online?

You need to know what they need to know. Once you understand their challenges, couple this with your expertise about how they can solve their challenges and from this will come your lead magnets.

Once you've got your 'need to knows', you then turn them into what we call lead magnets: purposefully built educational material designed to educate your target market on what they need to be doing in order to achieve the outcome they're looking for.

A lead magnet might be a book, a blog post, an e-book, an educational video or video series, it could be an e-learning program that people can sign up to for free and gain access to an education program on your website.

Your lead magnet should take into account three factors. I have adapted these three factors from a model originally taught to me by a great friend, Matt Church. Matt Church is 'the experts' expert', helping people take what's in their head and share it with the world.

The three factors are:

- *Market:* Who is my market and what do they want to know?

- *Message:* Once I know the market, what is my message?

- *Medium:* Given that I understand my market and have my message, how does my market want to receive this information (book, e-book, video, white paper, monthly updates)?

Often, if a strategic partner's customer list is big enough, the marketing departments in my businesses will create lead magnets completely tailored for that strategic partner, once we understand what the contacts on their list are looking for. If an offer is going out to 70 000 people, and our putting together a video series or an e-book can improve our results from an uptake of seven to an uptake of 1600, then the time needed for producing the video series is very well spent.

What lead magnets could you create to educate and entertain your target audience?

Creating strategic partnerships and the lead magnets that go with them should be the top priority for early-stage business owners. The greater the distribution you can reach through your partners and the better your lead magnets, the more people will know about you and the more people will want to buy from you.

Creating world-class strategic partnerships is just the first step in creating an attraction model. Let's talk about another way you can build your brand for free, by leveraging the media.

build your brand through the media

The difference between having a profile in the media as an entrepreneur and not having a profile can be like the difference between night and day. As a start-up business owner you need to put yourself where opportunity can see you.

When you're still a relatively unknown start-up, you have to push for everything: clients, partners, staff, suppliers, investors. However, once you start to build your profile through the media and people recognise you and identify with your brand, all of those people, such as clients, partners and investors, start to find you. You will still need to push — the effort never stops — but it does become easier to do business once you have the credibility and recognition that comes with building your personal profile and the brand of your business.

As an entrepreneur, if you can learn how to package a news story in such a way that the media are literally fighting over who gets the exclusive, you will not only be far more visible than anyone else in your industry, but you will also build the trust and following of your target market. And best of all? It's free.

Public relations (PR) is all about being the exception to the rule. The fact that you are in business for yourself means that you already stand out — you are already unique. However, this alone is not enough.

Journalists and media producers are bombarded every single day with press releases that are all about the individual or are focused on promoting the person's business. This isn't good enough if you want your story to run in the media. First, the story needs to be relevant to their readers or viewers, and second, the story can't be blatant promotion or else they will divert you to the advertising department.

Before you send out your press release, the story needs to be:

- *Relevant*—it's not all about you.
- *Factual*—it's not just an opinion.
- *Credible*—the argument makes sense and is coming from a reliable source.

Like anything in business, there is a right way and a wrong way to get noticed in the media. Let's look at the right way, which has enabled my clients and me to get hundreds of thousands of dollars of free PR every year over the last few years.

make it relevant—it's not about you

Instead of writing about yourself and what you have done, you need to find an existing issue to talk about in your press release.

The worst thing we can do is send out a press release that reads something like this:

> XYZ Company has recently released a new product that XYZ Company believes is going to revolutionise ABC industry because the market has never seen a JKL that does quite what this JKL does. If you'd like to speak to XYZ Company (about XYZ Company) then you can call us on ...

The problem with this example is that it is completely focused on the business. There are two issues here: the first is that it will be seen as an advertisement, rather than journalistic news; the second is that unless the business is currently at the centre of an existing major news story, it lacks relevance for the reader. Journalists would read the above example and be left thinking, 'Who cares?'

Great press releases leverage off an existing issue that is topical in the media. The issue should be relevant in the media *right now*, topical and even controversial — something that readers and viewers will identify with the minute they see the headline.

When we were starting The Entourage in 2010, we wanted to reach our audience of young entrepreneurs in Australia quickly. One of the ways we did this was to leverage the media to rapidly build our brand and our database.

At the time, Gen Y was topical in the media. Headlines like 'Who'd hire a Gen Y?' and 'Why bosses hate Gen Y' littered the media with opinions, facts and stats that media companies had collected.

We had heard from corporates; we had heard from government; and we had even heard the opinions of journalists as to why Gen Y was 'lazy, disloyal and unfocused'. Yet we hadn't heard from one party that was involved in all of this: Gen Y!

We decided to do some research of our own.

We ran a series of roundtables with the New South Wales state government of the time. I hosted each one, and we had guest speeches from the minister for small business. We attracted hundreds of Gen Ys into conference rooms in an initiative that stretched across New South Wales, giving Gen Ys a voice about what they believed they needed by way of support in order to be successful as career professionals or business owners.

A vast number of great insights came out of that exercise, both for me personally and for the government of the time.

The most notable finding for me — as a university dropout at the time — was the result of our request to participants to rate their university degree from 1–10, in terms of its effectiveness in preparing them for the business world. Universities came out with an average score of three out of

10—this highlighted a real gap in the traditional education system for Gen Ys.

We had clearly found a newsworthy issue. It wasn't about Jack or The Entourage or even the government; it was about how career-ready Gen Ys felt when they enter the workforce.

During the period of the roundtables and over the following weeks, we were featured in all the major newspapers, local newspapers, radio stations and major news networks, including Channel Ten Prime Time News and Channel Nine Prime Time News. I still remember standing next to the New South Wales minister for small business of the time, as we were being interviewed by Channel Nine News. He was asked, 'Do you think Gen Y will ever be successful in business?' After being surrounded by so many ambitious and inspiring Gen Ys for the past few days he promptly replied, 'They already are.'

Not long after, I went for the first time to a proper sit-down interview on a talk show. I had to be at the Channel Seven studios in Sydney at 5.40 am so they could do their best to make me look good before I had a live, on-air interview with Andrew O'Keefe on *Sunrise*—Kochie, the usual host, was away skiing that week.

I was nervous and tired, and had no idea what to expect. After make-up and 40 minutes of sitting around in the foyer, they walked me into the studio where the lights were so bright my eyes had to adjust to being in the room. Everyone in front of the camera was wearing suits and make-up, while behind the camera it was strictly torn jeans, flannelettes, bad shoes and take-away coffee.

As they cut for commercial, Andrew O'Keefe walked away from the news desk and over to a couch where they also directed me to go. The cameras, the crew and the lights all turned around as if on cue and were now solely focused on the couch with Andrew and me.

What was a four-minute interview seemed like it took 10 seconds. Andrew was incredibly kind and hospitable, and best of all was very easy to talk to. As they cut to the next segment Andrew and I shook hands, had a quick chat and wished each other well. Twelve seconds later I was standing out on Elizabeth Street in Sydney, alone, in the dark and feeling like I had just been ushered through a very well-engineered production line.

Such is media.

I had been invited that morning to talk about some of our findings with regards to Gen Y and the traditional education system, namely universities. The press release we sent them was so full of facts and stats, straight from the source, that it wasn't an opinion piece but factual data that the media were now starting to take notice of.

Throughout my business career, the media have played a pivotal role in building the brands of my businesses and my personal profile. After struggling to get noticed for years, the turning point for me was that, when I learnt how to package a story in a way that meant the media 'got it', we started to get traction with the media and build not only some great brands but also a great audience.

In the last 12 months these strategies have seen me featured in *GQ* magazine, *The Morning Show*, *Sky Business*, *BRW*, *Fitness First* magazine, *Ten News*, *The Sydney Morning Herald*, *The Age* and *Wealth Creator* magazine, allowing me to reach an audience of several million people, without my outlaying a cent. The art of a modern-day entrepreneur is to get noticed and build brand, even though we start with nothing—this is how we outplay the professionals.

make it factual, and not just an opinion—find the proof

Once you find the issue you're going to leverage off, you need to work out what your argument is in the context of that issue and find, or develop, facts and statistics to back up your argument. This can be achieved through research if you want to find existing information, or discovering new information, for example, by holding focus groups or circulating an online survey to people who have an interest in the issue.

The greater your sample size, the more credible your story will be. However, the research you do does not need to be of an academic standard. It doesn't need a sample size of thousands, it doesn't need to have the tick of approval of several university professors and it doesn't need to run through an 18-month bureaucratic process. Provided it is genuine information that is coming from real people and highlights a real issue, then it has enough integrity to be spoken about.

make it credible — be a reliable source

Be the messenger or be the example — ensure your story makes sense and that you can be trusted as a reliable source.

Once you've found the issue that you can leverage off, developed your facts and statistics to support the story, you have built permission to insert yourself into the story.

In this instance, if you're the messenger, then your press release will read something like:

> A recent survey conducted by The Entourage has highlighted that university students are dissatisfied with the level of education they're receiving while earning their degree. Jack Delosa, Executive Director of The Entourage, said that the findings of the survey highlight that students rated their university degree a three out of 10 in terms of its effectiveness in preparing them for the business world.

In this instance, The Entourage and I have developed the facts and stats, and I am simply the messenger.

However, sometimes you will be an example of what you're talking about and your press release will read something like this:

> One Gen Y who bucked the trend of university is Jack Delosa. At just 18 Jack Delosa decided to drop out of a commerce/law degree in order to develop his own business.

In this instance, I have been included in the story as an example of what we're talking about.

By being the messenger or an example, you're achieving two things. First, you have developed a broader story that is relevant to more people and is not just about you; second, you have still included yourself or your business in the story so that there is real tie-back value for you and your business.

Once you have found your issue, developed your facts and stats, and worked out how you're going to include yourself or your business in the story, it's then time to put pen to paper and write a press release that can be sent to media publications and television shows. This is where the real fun begins. Let's talk about how to write a press release that works.

how to write a press release that works

The structure of an effective press release is shown on the following page.

getting it out there

Once you have written your press release, it's important to remember the first rule of PR: be the exception to the rule.

The 'Submit a Story' tab on a website is not the way to submit a story. Nor is buying a list of 10000 journalists and sending them all a generic email about your story.

PRESS RELEASE

- IMPACTFUL HEADING -

PARAGRAPH 1
OUTLINE EXISTING ARGUMENT

PARAGRAPH 2
INTRODUCE YOUR **FACTS & STATS**

PARAGRAPH 3
EXPAND ON YOUR ARGUMENT

PARAGRAPH 4
QUOTES FROM YOU

PARAGRAPH 5
CLOSE WITH **WHY** THIS IS RELEVANT RIGHT NOW

CONTACT DETAILS:
YOUR NAME
PHONE NO
EMAIL
WEBSITE

TIP:
PRESS RELEASE
NO MORE THAN 3/4
OF THE PAGE!

Business is all about relationships, and that is especially true when it comes to building a good reputation in the media. Rather than spamming 10 000 journalists with a story that may or may not be appropriate for them, I would much rather build a great relationship with six to eight great journalists that I can call when I have a story, and who will call me when they need a quote on another story they're running. That way I can learn their style, I can build a profile of the kind of stories they love and I can work *with* them in producing great work.

You can always find a person's name. It might be that of the editor of a magazine you're looking for; it might be that of a particular journalist or columnist with a newspaper; or it might be the producer of a morning show.

If you are looking for a contact at a magazine, flick through the first few pages of the magazine and you will find a list of names, job titles, phone numbers and probably a generic email address. This is all the info you need to start.

If it's a newspaper, simply Google the person's name and chances are you'll be able to find a direct email for that person. You can also call the newspaper and ask for the person by name—not to talk to them about 'a press release', but to speak about 'a research project we've recently conducted that relates to the article they wrote in last week's newspaper'.

If it's a television show, then you'll be able to find the names of the producers and executive producers on the website and, same again, give them a call referencing a research piece you have recently completed that's relevant and topical in the media right now.

Once you have a name, phone number (even if it's generic) and an email address, do this:

1 Call them. The objective of this call is not to get them to say 'Yes, we'd love to run the story', but rather to have them say, 'Sure, shoot something over and I'll have

a look it.' Just this minor change in approach means that out of the hundreds of press releases they're going to receive that day, yours will be read.

2   Email them a personalised press release, entitled, for instance, 'For immediate release for *The Sydney Morning Herald*'. When talking about the current issue you're leveraging off, mention a specific article or piece they recently wrote that's relevant to that issue. Demonstrate that they're not one on a list of 10 000, and that you have done your research and understand them and their publication.

3   If you don't hear back within two days, give them another call. If they haven't responded, it's because they're not interested, they haven't read it, they were going to come back to you to ask for extra information and haven't had the chance yet or they love it and it's going to print or going to air next week. If they haven't looked at it, that's completely fine. Journalism is one of the busiest professions, so just let them know that you appreciate how busy they are and that you will wait to hear from them. If it's a 'no', then, without being pushy simply ask why: 'That's completely fine. Just so I can better tailor something for you next time, can I ask what didn't work for you with this particular story?' Journalists will always be more than happy to provide feedback, because hopefully it means next time you will send them a story they can run, and everyone wins.

I get how 'simple' this must sound. That's the point. Business was never meant to be complex—perhaps that's why so many successful business people are self-made, because they just found the simplest way to go from A to B and get the result. This simple formula—press release structure and strategy for getting it out there—has enabled us and our clients to generate hundreds of thousands of dollars in PR every single year. It works. Now you just need to work it.

Now that we've talked about building your brand for free through the media, let's talk about how you can become the go-to person in your industry by becoming a thought leader.

be the go-to person

Whether it be Richard Branson, who writes books, delivers keynote speeches and runs workshops on Necker Island each year; Jamie Oliver, who produces TV shows, writes cookbooks and delivers live onstage performances around the world; or Michelle Bridges, who by 2013 had authored eight books that sold half a million copies, created an online fitness program that had over 550 000 Facebook fans (Weight Watchers had 65 000), gained a regular spot on *The Biggest Loser* and brought in $67 million in product sales for the calendar year, each of these people have become thought leaders in their respective industries and are being paid handsomely as a result.

Thought leadership is the currency that builds your personal brand.

 @jackdelosa
Thought leadership is the currency that builds personal brand. #unprofessional

As we discussed earlier, regardless of what business you're in, you're in the business of education. You build brand and relationships by educating your audience on what they want, and you need to know about whatever it is they come to you for.

What do you know, perhaps even take for granted, that would make a difference to other people's lives if you were to teach them? What do you know that relates to your products or services that people want to be educated about?

You need to capture and release to your market your answers to those questions.

Capturing your message is about two things:

- standing for something
- picking a fight.

Branson stands for fun and adventure, and he's picked a fight with old and bureaucratic ways of doing things—often highlighting those features in his competitors, like British Airways and even Qantas. Jamie Oliver stands for great food, great company and creating magical moments with the people you love. Jamie has picked a fight with fast food and a system that is intent on not helping people get the nutritional education they need. Michelle Bridges stands for being the best you can be. She has picked a fight with traditional 'fad diets, saying, 'Guess what? They just don't work!'

The Entourage stands for creating success on your terms, whatever that might mean to you. We spend our time fighting an education system that is outdated and ineffective in today's business world.

What is your unique message? What is your fight?

Let's turn it up and get it out to your audience.

own your audience

In the past, if you wanted to reach a large audience, you would have needed a large advertising budget. TV, newspapers, magazines and any other mainstream media was the channel through which you could reach an audience. In order to access these big channels, you needed a lot of money, something you don't have a lot of when you're starting a business.

The internet has changed all that. Now anybody, anywhere, can build their own audience and communicate with them in their own voice to develop a strong relationship.

In an early-stage business, it's critical that you start to build your list of qualified prospects in your target market. Initially, a few hundred people may opt in to your database, then it will become thousands of people. When developed correctly, your customer list should develop into a database of hundreds of thousands of people over time. That gives you a captive audience of people who have opted in to your community that you can communicate with, add value to, solve problems for and sell to.

To own an audience, particularly a large audience, is one of the greatest assets you can have as a small- to medium-sized business. Once you own the audience, it's important that you continually add value to that audience through, for example, regular blog posts. These might be short posts, checklists, videos, how-to guides and other things that add value to your community, while positioning you as the go-to person for solutions in your industry — the person the media turn to when they need a comment on your established area of expertise.

KEYS TO OWN YOUR AUDIENCE

➤ Build your list through opt-ins — collecting names, email addresses, mobile numbers and any other information you need to build a relationship with that person.

➤ Achieve recency and frequency (see the next section) with that list, by adding value to the audience on a weekly basis through regular blog posts, videos, checklists and other resources that solve their problems.

➤ Understand that this database is your biggest asset. Without over-marketing to them, occasionally send exclusive promotional offers and incentives that drive them back to your online store, into your shop or just to an enquiry page where they can buy or download something of value to them.

Through The Entourage, we have implemented this strategy across cafés, tech companies, personal trainers, cupcake stores, PR companies, online fashion stores, corporate consultants and hundreds of other industries. In every case, it has worked to position the brand as a market leader and increase sales because it makes the company visible to more prospective customers.

Once you own the audience, every time you send out an email linking back to a blog post, lead magnet or a promotion of any sort, there will be a spike in website traffic, a spike in people coming into your shop, a spike in enquiries and ultimately a spike in revenue.

Better still, technology and the internet have made this incredibly easy and you can even do all of this for free.

Visit www.unprofessional.com.au/bonuses to see my recommendations for different database and email programs, where I outline which option is best for your business.

recency and frequency

It has been proven that when someone makes a buying decision, the brand that is front of mind is the brand that has communicated with them the most recently and the most frequently.

The benefit of becoming a thought leader is that you can communicate with your audience on a weekly basis. When what you send them stops being direct marketing and starts being incredibly valuable content that gives them new solutions to the challenges you know they're facing, they will not only open your emails, watch your videos and visit your website, they will also start to identify you and your business as their front-of-mind solution.

Jane Lu, founder of ShowPony Fashion (recently rebranded to ShowPo Fashion) and a graduate of The Entourage Scalable and Saleable Program, sells women's fashion online at a good price.

One of the first calls to action you see on Jane's home page is to 'Join Pony Club'. Notice it doesn't say 'Subscribe to Our Newsletter'. The last thing anyone needs is another weekly, fortnightly or monthly newsletter in their inbox, bringing dry, unimaginative content that serves no purpose other than to sell us something.

Jane's call to action reads: 'Sign up to be the first to hear about new styles, sales and random fun.' Jane lets her audience know that they will have first mover access to new styles; she gains permission to send promotions by mentioning sales, while also letting them know that ShowPo is a fun and edgy brand.

Jane knows that people often don't buy on their first visit to the website. By capturing their details and enlisting them for free into Pony Club, she is able to start building a relationship with the person over time through employing recency and frequency.

Google has also made recency and frequency achievable to those that don't opt in to your community or purchase on the first visit. Google Remarketing (www.google.com.au/ads/innovations/remarketing.html) allows you to continue marketing online messages to those people that have visited your site but haven't left their details. By installing a cookie on the user's computer, Google Remarketing will identify that they visited your site, and then display your ads when they visit other websites. This ensures that users usually see only messages that are relevant to them, while ensuring that your brand is in front of the people that have actively searched for it and are already familiar with you.

In order to achieve recency and frequency through building and educating your audience, ask yourself one question: 'What would I need to be *sending my audience* to have them *open* my emails *every week* in *anticipation?*'

When Jane Lu joined Scalable and Saleable she was generating impressive revenues of $40 000 per month. Now, just two short years later, she is consistently hitting $400 000 per month and growing. She is just 28.

developing great content that matters

When it comes to positioning your brand and building your profile as a thought leader, content is your currency and consistency is king. Although this principle is simple, anything that is easy to do is also easy not to do.

In order to add real value to your audience on a regular basis and thereby build a relationship with them, you need to publish and push out consistent and quality content every week. This might be a blog post, a video or a new lead magnet that solves a problem for your audience, or simply teaches them something that is of value to them.

Developing consistent quality content that speaks directly to your market and solves their problems can be difficult when you don't have a plan in place. If you have to think, strategise and write a new blog post or email every week while running a business, the running of the business will get in the way and you will end up writing a blog post once a month if you're lucky.

As a thought leader you should be publishing one blog post per week that provides useful content that will help your audience with whatever problems and challenges they are facing. This blog post might be a short article, it might be a checklist or it might be a video of you outlining certain how-tos for your audience to follow.

Rather than sitting down to produce content on a weekly basis, which can be very hard for most business owners, you should have a 12 Week Content Map in place. Your content map outlines every blog post, video or report you're going to publish for the next 12 weeks, and it allows you to do all of the thinking and developing at one time, and then publish each piece at the appointed time over the next 12 weeks.

Every 12 weeks you will plan the next 12 posts, documenting them in a structured plan, and then take half a day or a full day to write the articles, film the videos or develop the lead magnets. The hardest part of this is coming up with the topic, and deciding what to include and what not to include. Once this thinking is done and outlined in your Content Map, you will find the actual writing or recording will happens much more quickly, because you have done the thinking.

Adopt this strategy of building an audience, developing your message and consistently hitting recency and frequency with effective content and you will achieve a position of market leadership in your space.

Building an attraction is the most effective way to grow a start-up business. By creating strategic partnerships with complementary businesses, being recognised consistently in the media, and positioning yourself as the 'go to' person in your industry, you will be in a position where customers, partners and investors find you. Richard Branson is often quoted saying Virgin 'punch well above their weight' when it comes to the size of their brand relative to the size of their bottom line, meaning their brand is far bigger than their bottom line. As an early-stage entrepreneur, you too need to be punching above your weight and getting noticed on a much larger scale than what your bottom line might give you permission for.

Chapter 4

GET OVER YOUR FEAR OF SALES

The good news is that no-one likes to be sold to—in fact, selling died in the eighties. We all want to buy a car and own a car, but no-one wants to be *sold* a car. We'd love to buy a home and own a home, but we don't want to be *sold* a home.

Richard Branson said of Nelson Mandela that, above all, Mandela is a great salesperson. In his book *Business Stripped Bare*, Branson reflects that it is a very rare occurrence that he has dinner with Mandela without writing a cheque for upwards of $1 million. Branson argues that, whatever field you are in, the ability to influence and persuade people is the cornerstone of doing great things.

The good news is that anybody can learn how to be influential in business, simply by using the right strategies.

When Warren Buffett, the most revered investor in history, was 20 years old, he was socially inept: he preferred reading books to talking to people. But Buffett took Dale Carnegie's course, How to Win Friends and Influence People. He recognised that, if he was to attract capital from other investors, if he was to attract mentors to help him navigate the business world, if he was to attract great people to work with him and for him, he would have to become an effective communicator—someone people wanted to follow.

In an interview with the *Independent* newspaper in UK in 2009, Buffett reflected, 'You can't believe what I was like if I had to give a talk. I was so terrified that I just couldn't do it. I would throw up. In fact, I arranged my life so that I never had to get up in front of anybody.' He went on to talk about How to Win Friends and Influence People. 'It changed my life. I actually have the diploma hanging up in the office. And I don't have my diploma from college, I don't have my diploma from graduate school but I've got my Dale Carnegie diploma there because it changed my life.'

Be it in the business world, philanthropic space or even our personal life, learning to understand other people and ourselves on a deeper level makes us more effective people. It's not about being salesy or pushy—quite the opposite. It's about respecting other people and communicating with them in the way that *they* like to be communicated with, so that you can inspire and lead.

frame each conversation

We live in an age where people are silently begging to be led. Information is everywhere, but individuals and brands providing strong leadership are harder than ever to find.

Too many business owners let the prospect—the person in need of help and guidance—dictate the sales conversations and run their own process. This doesn't serve the potential customer, because it means that the business that can supply the help the prospect needs is providing very little leadership in the decision-making process. And it doesn't serve the business itself because it creates an unpredictable sales cycle, which means that the sales conversation might go for an hour, a week or in some cases even months. To install a successful sales process in your business you need to ensure there is as much consistency as possible.

At the beginning of each sales-based conversation it is critical that you or your sales team frame the conversation, giving the prospect the parameters of the conversation and what they can expect as an outcome. It is important to give the prospect on the other end of the telephone line, or sitting across the table, absolute clarity as to:

- *The purpose of the meeting and what you're chatting about.* For instance, you might start with: 'So today's really simple. It's just about me getting a good understanding as to where you're at with your [health and fitness, finances, accounting work, mobile phone—whatever business you are in] so that I'm able to best help you on what's going to be the best decision for you.'

- *The outcome of the discussion.* You might follow up with, 'Once we've had a bit of a chat we'll be in a position to make a decision together about [achieving the prospect's outcome] and you'll leave here with a good understanding of what the next steps are.'

An introduction like this demonstrates, first, that you're genuinely interested in the person you're speaking to and that the discussion is about *you* finding out about *them*, not about you selling them something. And, second, it demonstrates professionalism because you are showing you have a sales process and you're confident in taking the reins and leading the way.

ask the right questions

When most business owners or salespeople go into a sales environment, unfortunately they go straight into 'tell mode'. Telling the prospect about their products, blurting out all the features, all the different benefits and probably flying through the price and the different payment options.

The problem is when we tell we sell, and no-one likes to be sold to.

The biggest challenge for any salesperson or entrepreneur becomes how to sell without being 'salesy' by asking the right questions and helping your customers to buy.

At the beginning of a conversation chances are we don't know what the prospect needs. We don't know their situation, their objective in talking with us or the problem they're trying to solve, and therefore we're not yet in a position to *tell* them anything. Doing so simply makes us another salesperson who tried to sell them a product or service.

If, instead, you can take a genuine interest in the person, and take the time to understand where they are at and help them identify what they need, then you will be someone who has built rapport, taken an interest and helped them find a solution. You will be the exception to the rule.

Asking the right questions is all about having the prospect tell you why they need this solution, rather than you telling them. If you say why they need the solution, the prospect can doubt it; if the prospect says it, it's true. Becoming a master of asking the right questions is about helping people feel comfortable enough to let you into their situation, desires and challenges. Once you can achieve this genuine connection with another person, you have permission to ask them the questions required to determine whether they have a real need for your product or not.

Throughout the early years of my career, I searched relentlessly for a system to help me ask the right questions—a model that I could use and that I could train sales teams to utilise in order to give them direction in asking the right questions so they could get the best result in the shortest amount of time.

After trying out all sorts of systems, I found they were too complicated and so the model couldn't be followed in a way that was easy and conversational. So I decided to create my own. This is an insanely simple, yet profound, method of structuring your questions so that they follow a comfortable line of thought and help both the prospect and you fully understand where they are and what they need.

We don't just use the model for selling products, we also use it to create partnerships and network, and bring it into play in any other situation where we are negotiating with another person. I call it SOAR.

SOAR

➤ **S**ituation—Ask them questions to identify where they are now in relation to their problem and the solution they seek.

➤ **O**bjective—Ask them questions to identify what their desired outcome is.

➤ **A**ny challenges—Ask them questions that will help them identify what has been stopping them from getting this outcome.

➤ **R**esults—Outline how you can help them get what they want, using the language they have used throughout the conversation.

SOAR—asking the right questions in sales

The sample questions in table 4.1 are hypothetically for a client who has come to see you to help them raise money from investors.

Table 4.1: sample questions for a client looking for help in raising money from investors

SOAR	Summary	Explanation	Example questions	Your energy
1 Situation	Where are they now?	To begin with, ask questions that help you and them understand their current situation relative to what they have come to you for.	'How's business at the moment?' 'Are you guys experiencing some good growth?'	Friendly
2 Objectives	Where do they want to be?	Once you understand their situation, ask questions that help you understand their objectives.	'How much money do you want to raise?' 'What would you like to do with that money?'	Interested
3 Any challenges	What's stopping them?	Once they've reflected on their objectives, they should be comfortable in articulating what problems they have had in achieving their objectives. This is very important, as it is probably the reason they have come to see you.	'Have you been trying to raise the money yourself?' 'What challenges have you had so far?'	Empathetic
4 Result	What would you prescribe?	This is where you stop asking questions and start diagnosing the problem and articulating what you believe the person needs to do in order to overcome their challenge and achieve their objective. If there is a genuine need, this is where you talk about your product or service.	'Okay, thank you very much for that, I think I have enough information to make an informed decision about what you need to do. The first step is going to be . . .'	Authoritative

provide a solution

If a prospect has taken the time to talk with you and explain their objectives and challenges, they are doing so because they want you to present a suitable solution. This is where you need to be the thought leader and, like a doctor writing a prescription, explain to the person what they need to do and why. This solution, of course, may involve getting started with you and doing business together or, if you decide that you are not the best solution for them, it may simply involve pointing them in the right direction.

If you do believe you can help the prospect overcome their challenges and achieve their objectives, then you need to present your solution in a way that is completely tailored for them.

Forget about all the features of your product or service, and the things you think are important. What do *they* think is important? That's what you need to focus on.

In giving them a quick overview of your product or service you do so in a tailored manner, relating the product or service back to their situation, objectives and challenges every step of the way. You need to present the information in such a tailored way that the prospect understands it is exactly what they need and that it will help their personal situation. Tailoring the conversation to the prospect's needs ensures you are not talking *at* them about another 'off-the-shelf' product, which is probably what they were offered by the last three people they spoke to. Instead, you are presenting them with a tailored solution that will help them overcome the challenges they have just told us about.

get their buy-in

It is important that, even though this is the part where you are the one doing most of the talking, you still check in with them each step of the way to ensure that they are engaged in what you're talking about. You can achieve this by simply pausing and asking questions like, 'Is that something you think would make a difference?' And, 'Do you see how that will help you achieve what you're looking for?' Getting mini buy-ins throughout the tour will ensure the prospect is with you every step of the way.

new words for 'closing the sale'

Many sales are lost because the salesperson doesn't ask for the business.

If someone has invested time with you and trusted you enough to share the details of their situation, then chances are they probably want to buy from you. Now all that's required is your leadership to outline what the next steps are and how they can get started.

It is important that during this process you don't use ugly sales words that might turn the prospect off or have them ask for time to 'go away and think about it'. Provided we've framed the conversation, asked the right questions and demonstrated the right value, we now have permission to help get them started.

The language we use, particularly in a sales environment, will greatly affect the person we're speaking to, and therefore how comfortable they are in moving ahead with us. Here are some words that we don't use and what we say instead (see table 4.2, overleaf).

Table 4.2: changing your language to help your customers buy more easily

Old words	Problem	New words
How would you like to pay?	The word 'pay' often has negative associations and brings up any money issues. Remove this problem by changing your wording.	How would you like to fix that up/take care of that/ sort that out?
We'll just go through the contract.	No-one (no-one!) likes contracts. They sound so legal and binding and scary.	Too easy, now all we need to do is fill out a little bit of paperwork ...
You'll be locked in for 12 months ...	No-one wants to be locked in: it makes us feel restricted, probably in much the same way as a contract.	It's just a 12-month plan ...
I just need to finalise the sale.	It's not about you 'closing' a sale, it's about helping the person get started with what is going to solve their challenges.	Let's get you started ...
No, we don't do that ...	'No' sounds like a dead-end and implies that you're not flexible. Rather than telling a prospect what you *don't* do, tell them what you *do*.	What we've found with our existing clients is what works even better than that is ... [state what you *can* do]

getting started sequence

When you're at the business end of the conversation, it's crucial you understand exactly where you're going to take the conversation. This means developing your getting started sequence. This may vary slightly from business to business, but the principles at large will be fairly consistent.

1   Often the best way to get started is to present the prospect with two different options and ask which they are more interested in: 'So which do you think would suit your lifestyle better, the personal training or the outdoor group classes?'

2 Ask if they'd like to get started: 'Brilliant! And is that something that you'd like me to help you get started with today?'

3 Give them two options for taking care of payment: 'And how did you want to fix that up, cash or credit?'

4 Help them with the paperwork: 'Too easy, we can do that. What we need to do now to get you started is just take care of a little bit of paperwork.'

5 Outline the next steps. As discussed earlier, this helps them understand they are dealing with an experienced professional who isn't afraid to guide them on the right path. 'From here, what's going to happen is that you'll receive ...'

6 Reassure them. Have them articulate to you the reasons why they're getting started today: 'As discussed, given your [situation/objectives/challenges], I think this is going to work well for you. Are you excited?' [Await response] 'What excites you the most?'

Having models to follow when asking the right questions, providing a solution and getting people started means that you will not only have the skills but also the confidence to walk people through any negotiation or sales process. Remember, regardless of what you're selling, ultimately what you're providing is a solution to a problem that the customer has. Provide the right leadership throughout this process and you won't have won a customer, you will have created a relationship.

people crave 'real'

Gone are the days where you would have a 'work you' and a 'real you'. In today's business world they are one and the same. If you're a business owner, there is very little separation between your brand and your true self.

I believe there are two implications to this new reality and that both are conducive to better business.

The first is that we cannot be one thing and pretend to be something else. We cannot be a timid person building an audacious brand with an adventurous culture—people both inside and outside the organisation will see through it.

In the 21st century, most people have an incredibly accurate BS filter, and anything that is not genuine, and not congruent with who you truly are, will be highlighted and protested against.

The second is that the new reality gives us permission to be ourselves at all times. This does not mean that we don't push ourselves to work hard, it doesn't mean that we don't present a great brand to the market and it doesn't mean that we can relax to the extent of being unprepared or lazy. It simply means that while being the best version of ourselves, we have permission to be real.

Whether it be in a sales environment, partnership discussion, capital raising or recruitment process, everyone you speak to is a human being and will appreciate honesty, transparency and a human element to the conversation. This accelerates and strengthens the development of relationships.

It can be scary at first, but once you start to drop the mask, you'll be surprised how fast it falls to the ground.

> @jackdelosa
> Once you start to drop the mask, you'll be surprised how fast it falls to the ground.
> #uprofessional

prove it

When you go to online retailer Ruslan Kogan's website, kogan.com, two things happen.

First, boxes start appearing in the bottom left-hand corner with a suburb, and the name of the product they have just purchased. Given Kogan's sales volumes, the minute one box fades away, another appears in its place with a new suburb and a new product someone there has just purchased. You can also click on the link to the product and it will take you straight to that product's sales page.

The second thing that happens is that the screen darkens and a bright white box pops up in the middle of the screen suggesting that you should like the Kogan Facebook page to get access to their exclusive Facebook offers and promotions. It also tells you how many other people have already liked this page, giving you confidence that this is an established business with an existing tribe.

So often when a prospect is about to make a buying decision they hesitate, because what will happen on the other side of the purchase is unknown. They will pause, think about it and maybe even second guess the purchase, even if it is the very thing they need. If they haven't bought from you before, questions will be circling in their mind about whether this is the right purchase, whether you are the right business, whether you will deliver on what the glossy marketing promises, even whether now is the right time for this purchase.

To overcome these problems, in any sales process the most effective tool you can use is *social proof*: showing the prospect that other people have already made this decision and are glad they did.

Whether it be face-to-face, over the phone or online, being able to showcase success stories from those that have bought from you and loved the experience will give your prospect the social proof they need to confidently make a buying decision.

The Kogan website also has a 'Reviews' page, which features articles from different media reviewing Kogan's products. In one review *The Daily Telegraph* remarks, 'A giant screen seems like a luxury until you try one. By then you'll be convinced it's one of life's essentials.' Having comments and experiences written by people and recognised media is a great way to establish social proof and trust with your brand.

Often when people have had a great experience with your brand they are more than happy to provide you with a testimonial outlining how they found the experience and talking about the benefits of using your product. Most testimonials will be prepared as either a written case study or a quick video from the customer outlining the experience they have had—usually a combination of the two works best to accommodate different communication styles.

However, like everything in business, there is a right way and a wrong way to producing testimonials.

A great testimonial will meet the following criteria:

- *The 'before shot'*. This is where the customer outlines what their situation was like before, what their challenge was and what their frustrations were. For example, 'A giant screen used to seem like a luxury.'

- *Something changed*. There was a moment when they bought a product, or started a program, or met a person who changed that situation and enabled them to find a solution to their problem. For instance, 'I tried the even bigger screen.'

- *The 'after shot'*. This is what they've achieved since they bought your product or service. If this is about acquiring a simple product, a testimonial might just be a simple explanation of what it does for them and the ease of use. If you're an accountant or a personal trainer, you want your client to get very specific about what they achieved and over what time frame—you want them to mention specific use numbers, percentages and milestones reached. For instance, 'I've become so acquainted with my new screen that it's now one of my life's essentials.'

Once you have acquired some testimonials, scatter references to them throughout your sales process, both in written and video form—they should appear on your website, on your sales pages, in your videos, in your brochures and in your sales collateral.

As human beings, our instinct to follow the tribe is still very strong, especially when we're hesitant and afraid of making the wrong decision. Having powerful testimonials strategically placed throughout your sales and marketing material will enable a much smoother conversation or transaction when it comes time for the person to purchase.

Founded in 2006, Kogan Technologies has been a *BRW* Fast 100 Company every year since 2009, and the company had an estimated revenue of $75.2 million in 2012. By the time you read this, every figure in this case study will have grown and almost all of the features I have outlined on the website will have changed. Ruslan Kogan is an innovator who is forever challenging the status quo and innovating his way forward.

what to do 80 per cent of the time

For early-stage businesses the most important ingredient is cash. We need to ensure that there is cash in the bank and cash coming in at all times. With it we can invest, recruit and reach further; without it, our days are numbered.

Research shows that the average small-business owner spends 11 per cent of their time on revenue-generating activities; however, as an early-stage business owner you need to spend a minimum of 80 per cent of your time on revenue-generating activities.

These activities include sales, marketing, creating partnerships, developing lead magnets, testing, measuring and iterating any form of outreach that brings customers into the business and cash into the bank.

Through The Entourage we speak to more than 10 000 business owners every single year, and I can tell you that the companies that are profitable and growing are the ones that are led by a sales-focused entrepreneur. For struggling businesses, on the other hand, it doesn't matter how clever their marketing campaigns are or how effective their sales process is—if the energy and the time aren't being put in, that business will either not survive or, even worse, it will plod along for years giving the owners just enough cash flow to live on.

One of my best friends and a man I respect very much is Andrew Morello, known affectionately to his friends as Morello. Morello won the first Australian season of *The Apprentice* television program, hosted by Mark Bouris, who sold Wizard Home Loans to GE for $500 million. Upon winning *The Apprentice*, Morello was immediately hired by Bouris and to this day remains head of business development at Yellow Brick Road, a company Bouris started to bring good financial advice to everyday Australians.

Morello is a person who lives and breathes business development—he calls it 'shaking hands and kissing babies'. When there's a deal that needs to be closed, a conflict that needs to be resolved, an enquiry that needs to be addressed, Morello is the person that Yellow Brick Road fly around the country to make it happen. Most mornings he's on the first plane at 5 am, and it's not uncommon for him to be in three states on any given day. Chances are he won't stop until 10 pm.

People who observe Morello's output and work ethic often ask the question, 'How does he get so much done?' Morello's response is profoundly simple. He lives according to what he calls his 'ideal week'. He has broken his annual sales target into quarters, broken the quarterly targets into months, the monthly targets into weeks and the weekly targets into days. This is a man who knows exactly what he must do every single day in order to succeed in his role.

It doesn't stop there. He also knows how many calls he needs to make in order to get a meeting, how many meetings he needs to get an application and how many applications he needs to sign on a new Yellow Brick Road branch.

Knowing his targets and understanding his numbers means that Morello knows how much time he needs to dedicate to calls, meetings, networking, speaking on stage and other business development activities every week. He therefore templates the amount of time he will spend on the different activities each week and in doing so ensures he spends the right amount of time doing the right things—he is both efficient and effective.

Today, Morello, at the age of 27, has helped build Yellow Brick Road into a public company with more than 170 branches and a market capitalisation (value) of $126 million by 2013.

To match Morello's success, you need to start with identifying your targets. What sort of sales target or revenue target could you set for yourself for the coming 12 months? What are the core activities you need to be doing on a weekly basis to ensure you hit your targets? What does your ideal week look like?

vital signs and business health

In hospital wards the world over there are people lying on hospital beds with a clipboard at the end of the bed. Numbers that are consistent across these clipboards are things like a patient's heart rate, breathing rate, temperature and blood pressure. These numbers are so critical to the health of a patient that they are regularly and rigorously measured, monitored and managed.

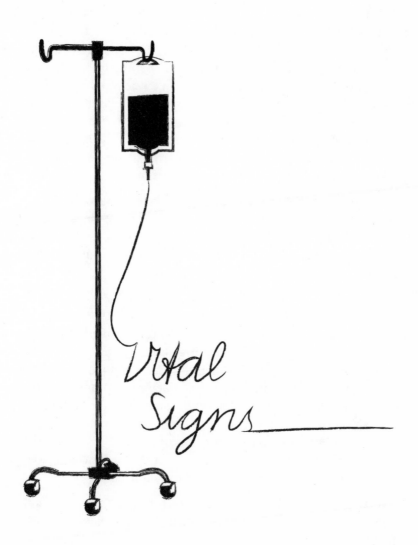

Vital
Signs_____

Business is no different. In every business there are certain numbers that, when effectively measured, monitored and managed, can accurately reflect the overall health of the business.

Unfortunately, the vast majority of early-stage businesses do not actively strategise and assess the vital signs across the company. This means that the owner, the CEO and the people within the business don't know what success looks like, let alone whether they're achieving it or not. This results in a lack of leadership, a lack of clarity around the direction of the business and a lack of accountability within the business. Without all of these factors working together, a business simply cannot survive.

Vital signs are not only important at a business management level; it is also critical for every person in the organisation to have targets and numbers that are relevant to their role. Even if you're a sole proprietor just setting out on your journey, you need to know the vital signs that you measure each week to ensure your personal performance is in line with what you are setting out to achieve.

The vital signs for a business development manager might be the number of calls made, meetings conducted, applications received and sales made. For an online marketing manager, the vital signs might be the number of database opt-ins, amount of social media growth, email open-rates, click-through rates, overall web traffic and conversion rates of any sales pages. For an operations manager, the vital signs might include tasks completed, projects progressed, operational errors made, reports received and a customer satisfaction rating.

Every person in every one of our businesses has vital signs that are measured and reported, on a weekly basis, to the CEO.

Every Tuesday afternoon before 5 pm, each of the managers in our businesses submit their vital signs report to our CEO. After reviewing the vital signs on the Tuesday night, the

CEO then meets individually with every manager across their company for 30 minutes to discuss their vital signs, identify where the manager believes they are strong, what areas need improvement and what the CEO or board can do to better support and enable the success of that individual.

This not only ensures that every person within each business understands they are accountable to certain targets, but also means they feel supported, because the CEO of the business is taking an active interest in their success on a weekly basis and allowing them to be heard.

The CEO then submits his or her vital signs to the board of directors once a month at a board meeting. The CEO's vital signs include all the numbers that are critical to the overall health of the business. This will include things like a profit and loss statement for the month (we will discuss this more in chapter 7—'Know your numbers'), number of new customers acquired and customers lost, cash at bank, accounts receivable, accounts payable, sales pipeline and any other figures that are important for the ongoing success of the business.

If you're running a business with staff and a management team, then your vital signs will look something like those I have just outlined. If you're just getting started and you're still tackling the mountain by yourself at this stage of the game, then you need to set vital signs for yourself personally to achieve each week and ensure that you are reviewing them weekly. These vital signs meetings, even if it is a meeting conducted with yourself, should appear in your calendar as part of your 'ideal week'.

generating referrals

In acquiring new customers, nothing is more powerful than friends recommending you to friends. In most great businesses, this happens naturally: a customer has a great experience and goes on to talk about you to their network.

When someone has been referred to you by a friend that they like and trust, most of the relationship-building process has been done for you, because they are coming to you from a known and trusted source. Eighty per cent of the work has been done before you even speak to them.

The opportunity is then for every great business not to wait for referrals to happen reactively, but to invite and even incentivise happy customers to tell their friends.

Referrals should be generated at the peak of the customer journey. Look at your customer journey and ask yourself, 'At what point in this process is our customer happiest and most excited to be using us?' If you're an accountant, this might be after tax time when your clients receive their tax return. If you're a personal trainer, it might be once the client has reached their ideal weight. If you sell cupcakes, it's probably at the point of sale where the person has just bought their cupcake and you can give them a 'two for one' deal that they can pass on to their friends.

Referrals should never be about, 'Do you know anyone else that would like to buy our product?' but rather positioning the question around the experience the person has had or the result they have achieved.

For instance, in an accounting practice, rather than asking, 'Do you know anyone else who might want to use us?' (bland, boring), after tax time you should be asking, 'Who else do you know that would like to receive thousands of dollars from the tax man next July?' If you're a personal trainer it might be, 'Who else do you know that would love to be able to reach their ideal weight?' And if you're selling cupcakes, then it's a focus on the experience: 'If you know anyone else that loves cupcakes as much as you do, feel free to pass on this two for one offer.' Or, 'If you love cupcakes as much as we do, hide this two for one offer from your friends and feel free to use it yourself next time!' Chances are when they come back it will be with friends.

Communicating like a professional, asking the right questions and providing the right information will all add up to one thing: helping your customer buy more from you more often. It's not about 'selling'; it's about providing the necessary leadership to enable your customers to buy.

Early-stage businesses that have an effective sales process and produce the necessary proof and reassurance along the way will far outperform organisations that are stuck in the old ways of talking customers through product features.

Chapter 5

BECOME NUMBER ONE ONLINE

The internet has not only levelled the playing field, but it has also meant that in the online world smaller businesses now have a real advantage over larger businesses when it comes to speaking to the hearts and minds of their consumers and building a relationship with their market.

While corporations and big businesses are spending up to four weeks to get one Facebook post for their fan page approved by their legal team, smaller businesses are speaking, in a real tone, to their customers and potential customers every single day. Social media and email communication have meant that it is easier and more effective than ever before to achieve recency and frequency with your audience.

In addition, more than ever before, anyone can acquire customers and build relationships relatively easily and quickly by implementing the right online strategies. No longer do you need to run a television commercial or an ad in a newspaper to reach your market: you can now use the online world to build your own audience and speak directly to them in the tone of your brand.

The brand that best harnesses email marketing, social media and effective online strategies will outperform the customer acquisition of any larger business, which probably still has its hands tied behind its back in bureaucracy and legal protocol.

A world-class online strategy will achieve three things:

- *Inspire*. Make sure you are visible and relevant, releasing content that 'speaks' to your audience.

- *Capture*. Give your audience an incentive to opt in to your database on their first visit so that you can start building a relationship with them.

- *Nurture*. Continue to communicate with your audience and add value for them in a way that strengthens the relationship further.

inspire, capture, nurture

To *inspire* your audience online you need to regularly release content that educates your audience about what they need to know, entertains your audience or does things that bring your brand to life. Inspire is about amplifying content that will speak to the hearts and minds of your audience through email or social media, be it through releasing lead magnets, posting interesting facts or ideas, or asking questions that will get your audience engaged. Keep it fun, interesting and relevant.

To *capture* your audience you need to communicate your value proposition in one short sentence and give people a strong reason to opt in to your community, so that you can capture their details for your database and start building a relationship with them—more on this on page 100.

inspire		
LEAD MAGNETS	BLOG POSTS	SOCIAL MEDIA
PARTNERS	VIDEO	PR

capture		
OPT IN	FREE TRIAL	BUY

nurture		
REGULAR EMAILS	SOCIAL MEDIA	USEFUL CONTENT

> **TIP**
>
> Your value proposition is how you communicate the benefit of what you do to your customers. Through speaking with customers and gaining consumer insights, your value proposition should be deliberately crafted to speak straight to the hearts and minds of the people who matter most—your customer.

Once a person has opted in to become a part of your community, you need to nurture the relationship by regularly talking to them and adding value for them. This is achieved through recency and frequency—sending them educational or entertaining content that engages the user, whether through weekly updates, blog posts or videos, for example. Remember the process of nurturing is not about sending a newsletter once a month that outlines your new products or markets your new services; it's about adding value and educating your audience on what they want to know, like we discussed in chapter 3 in the section entitled 'recency and frequency' (see p. 55).

Whether you have a well-established online brand or are starting from scratch, you will find details in this chapter about how to grab your audience's attention and turn that into paying customers.

it's easier than ever before

It is easier than ever before to launch a social media campaign, send emails that really *speak* to your audience, and build a website that sells.

Let's look at the different components of your web strategy and some of the places you can go to get the job done quickly and effectively.

building or updating your website

You don't need to know how to 'code' or do any 'techy' stuff to build a website. Today anybody can quickly browse different themes and different layouts of pre-existing website structures to create a world-class website on a very lean budget.

Two companies in particular, Shopify.com and Wordpress .com, provide the templates and all the help you need to create your own website, without paying a fortune to an 'expert'.

Shopify is one of the best platforms in the world for any retail business. If you host a lot of products and need to manage stock, display products and whisk customers through an online checkout, then Shopify will do this. You can use Shopify.com to create a fully functional website, with e-commerce, blogging and all the reportability you need to launch an online store and have complete visibility over what's selling and where the money is coming from. It also allows you to choose from existing and customisable templates that look professional and very well designed, while optimising every page for search so that you can be found though search engines.

Shopify also integrates with Google Adwords, a program by Google that allows you to post ads in front of the people who are actively searching for what you're selling. In order to email your customers and remain front of mind, it also integrates with MailChimp, an online system that allows you to easily email your database or segments of your database.

If you're looking to build a website that isn't necessarily geared toward online retail, Wordpress.com will also allow you to create a fully functional and well-designed website using existing templates that work. Wordpress is a great platform for hosting your website blogging and regularly updating your website content.

manage and communicate with your customers

To remember, manage and communicate with every single one of your customers, you need a customer relationship manager (CRM) system that allows you to track the behaviour of your customers and potential customers, and keep notes on each of them. This represents real value to any business trying to speak to its consumers, because it allows you to personalise the different messages you send out, according to each person's past behaviour. Your CRM must include an email marketing system that allows you to email and text your audience regularly. This is where a simple email program like MailChimp will be incredibly useful.

MailChimp as a program allows you to send emails to your database or sections of it, and keep notes on clients, as well as tracking open rates for emails and click-through rates. It is a great solution for anyone on a tight budget wanting a simple place to start.

THREE LEVELS OF CRM SYSTEMS

---

1 Simple (1–2 staff): MailChimp

2 Mid-Ground (2–10 staff): OfficeAutopilot

3 Comprehensive (10+ staff): Salesforce

Note: The price goes up the more comprehensive the program, but all are affordable for early-stage businesses.

A more comprehensive CRM system is provided by officeautopilot.com. It is more sophisticated than mailchimp .com and offers more features. OfficeAutoPilot includes a CRM system, an email marketing system, a web payment processor, an auto-responder marketing system that includes 'if–then' rules ('if a prospect does this, then send them that'), affiliate tracking, lead scoring and event management.

It also integrates with Wordpress, allowing people to opt in to your community on your website, and their details will automatically be populated into your CRM in Office-AutoPilot. OfficeAutoPilot is cost effective for early-stage businesses and is charged as a monthly subscription.

A fully comprehensive system is provided by Salesforce .com. Considered one of the world's leading CRM systems, Salesforce does everything that OfficeAutoPilot does, plus more. It is generally used by larger businesses that need high-level functionality and customisation that is specific to their business. While you can learn how to use OfficeAuto-Pilot through some training videos, Salesforce is an option that requires a higher investment of both money and time to implement, but that will be worthwhile for larger businesses.

iterate and adapt

Just as we said in chapter 2, 'Start before you're ready', the online world should be a place of never-ending testing, measuring and improving.

I remember when Ruslan Kogan was speaking at one of our Young Entrepreneur Unconventions for The Entourage, Australia's largest event for entrepreneurs under 40, an audience member asked him to look at their website and say what he thought of it. Ruslan responded with, 'I don't even look at kogan.com and tell my team what I think. It shouldn't be about anyone's opinion but rather testing and finding out the facts.'

In today's economy, online marketing should be more of a science than an art because we can collect data and metrics so quickly and easily that everything we do and every change we make should be driven by user behaviour.

Marketing your business through an online web presence is useless without web pages that convert visitors into either subscribers or active prospects submitting an enquiry.

Sometimes the problem is that the awesome copy you have written on your site may not be compelling enough to convince your visitors to take action and submit an enquiry. But manually experimenting with different headlines and sales copy is time-consuming and difficult to manage. Instead, you can use A/B testing, a method of rapidly testing different page headlines and content and tracking the conversion rates—how many people who view the page actually opt in to the next step or buy. A/B testing can be used to quickly find what content is working, and where there are opportunities for improvement.

Let's say you have 'Compelling Headline 1' and 'Compelling Headline 2' as two variations of your homepage. Once A/B testing has been activated, the first visitor to your website (Visitor A), will be directed to your homepage with 'Compelling Headline 1', and the second visitor (Visitor B) will see 'Compelling Headline 2'. The third will see 'Compelling Headline 1', and so on. You can then track the number of enquiries from each of the two page variations and then direct all the traffic to the better-performing page. At this point you would create another variation of the homepage to start A/B testing it against the better-performing page.

Some content management systems (CMS), such as Wordpress, have A/B testing plugins available, or you may choose to fully host your site on an A/B testing platform, such as unbounce.com. A/B testing is a process of continuous improvement, and once you have 'split tested' a page and found out how to improve it, you can implement improvements and then test out other page elements, such as images, call-to-action buttons and even colours. If your opt-in rate increases from 3 per cent to 4 per cent, that's a 25 per cent growth in database acquisition—a significant gain from just some simple iterations.

> **TIP**
>
> A plugin is an add-on to an existing program that can be added with minimal hassle, usually at the press of a button.

the new SEO

Search engine optimisation (SEO) is about optimising your web presence so that your website appears high, preferably on page one, in the listings of search engines like Google when people search for keywords that match what you do.

Ask yourself, how many customers who are actively searching for what you're offering would you get in front of if you appeared first on Google for your relevant search terms?

Rather than spending money on blanket advertising that gets put in front of anybody regardless of what they might be looking for, an effective SEO strategy means that you appear front and centre to qualified prospective customers who are actively trying to find what you have. This can be hundreds of thousands and sometimes millions of people every single month.

To appear on the front page of Google for search terms relevant to your business is the busiest shopfront you will ever have.

> **TIP**
>
> To find what keywords people are searching for in your industry, and how competitive the keywords are, simply search for Google Keyword Planner and it will direct you through researching what people are searching for that is relevant to you and your business.

SEO has changed dramatically in recent years and it is always being updated and changed as search engines like Google strive to display more relevant results to their customers searching for information, while at the same time cutting down on ways that website owners can 'game the system' to artificially increase search results.

Many of the SEO strategies used to increase rankings that worked in years past are now actually *penalised* by Google and other search engines because of their overuse. There is, however, a common theme, which has not changed, and that is that Google and the other search engines are always striving to display the *most relevant* content to their customers. This means that for your website to rank better, you need to be producing *original, relevant, engaging* content.

The most effective content you can produce and publish on your website is now videos and blog posts. These should be of value to your website visitors and be *original* content. If Google reads your website content (as its 'crawlers' browse the web to update its index) and discovers that it has already been published elsewhere, Google will not count it as original content, and may even down-rank your site if it believes the content is spam or of poor quality.

Beware of so-called SEO experts touting increased rankings from any of the following outdated methods, as they will now directly hurt your rankings:

- *backlinking*—having other companies link to your website purely for the sake of creating more links

- *link-farms*—a set of web pages created for the sole purpose of linking to a certain web page

- *classifieds posting*—creating classified ads online for the purpose of SEO.

content is king

As we discussed in chapter 3, 'Build an attraction model', regular blog posts are the easiest and yet most effective way to regularly produce new content that will boost your Google ranking. Your posts must focus on the customer, not you or your business. They will focus on what your customers need to know, customer testimonials and your thought leadership opinion pieces.

A great source of ideas for your blog posts is customer enquiries. Have you written down a list of the questions your customers typically ask when purchasing your product? Or the objections they raise or reasons they give for not buying your product or service? Inherent in these objections will be your customers' FAQs, concerns and roadblocks, which, once answered, enable them to make a buying decision.

These are great starting blocks for education blog posts and articles, as they deal with customer questions and objections up-front. Your posts may help to reduce buyer resistance if and when a prospect decides to buy from you down the track.

Tackle just one question or objection per blog post. If you're putting forward a new argument and challenging the status quo, make sure your argument is well reasoned, supported by evidence and an expression of your opinion—not a declaration of the truth according to you. Remember your aim is to *inspire* prospects to do business with you—not scare them away.

Alongside your own posts, you may also include guest posts from a non-competing, complementary business that can help educate your client base in a way that enhances your own brand. Your guest blog posts should be aimed at the same audience, and 'on message' with what you are educating your clients about and the action you want them to take. Just keep in mind that if guest content is not consistent with your own, you run the risk of diverting your prospects' attention away from your site and your message.

video that works

When you are vying for website traffic from the results of people searching for what you do, a compelling video on your homepage will greatly increase the page view time (viewed positively by the search engines) and increase the engagement of your website visitors.

Videos have been proven to enhance engagement, significantly improve conversion rates from prospect to customer and quickly build trust with your audience.

A video should outline the results or end benefit you provide to your customers, what makes your business unique and even include a call to action to direct viewers to engage with your business. Recording a homepage introduction video can be as simple as using a good-quality smartphone or HD video camera and basic editing software such as iMovie for Mac OS X. If you want a more professional look and feel, you can engage video production companies who will fully manage the whole process for you for a small budget, including script editing, filming and editing.

Posting videos to YouTube and your website will also help with your SEO and rankings, as Google sees video as relevant and unique content. Video helps contribute to your online identity and collection of published content that Google uses to determine how much of an authority you are on your particular area of expertise. The more *quality* video content you have produced and uploaded to YouTube, and the more views that content receives, the more weight Google will give your business name and online profile when ranking your site.

Google has also updated its search results page to include video results in-line with standard website results. If you are in a niche market or your videos are well targeted to popular keywords relevant to your business, your videos, both on YouTube and on your website, can now show up in standard search results. Sometimes video search results will also show up alongside your website—giving you two spots in Google's top 10 search results!

A simple video content marketing strategy for your business might be to record 10 videos, each two to three minutes long, on the most common questions prospects ask before engaging your services, followed by another 10 videos, of the same length, explaining the core things your audience needs to know about what you do.

Upload all of the videos to YouTube and then once per week embed them into a blog post on your website with a short summary. You can then share those blog posts on social media or link to them in your newsletter to reach a further audience, which also adds to your recency and frequency.

Supplementing your website, blog and SEO strategies with video content will help boost your rankings and credibility with customers, and will result in educated prospects calling your business, excited to do business with you.

One Entourage Scalable and Saleable Program Member, Peter Moriarty from IT consultancy firm itGenius, often educates his audience on how to automate their business using Google Apps. As a result of one video, his website now shows up on page one of Google results for anyone searching for exactly that, putting Peter front and centre in front of thousands of people actively searching every month for what he's offering.

increase your ranking even further

In addition to Google putting extra weight on unique and relevant content being generated for your website ranking, it now also heavily weights social interactions when choosing which pages to rank highest in their search results. It uses social interactions as a metric for measuring an article's popularity. The number of times a blog post or online article is shared on Twitter, Facebook or Google+ affects its ranking in Google search results.

This increases the stakes for content creators (of which you are one) to encourage you to produce content that's valuable enough for your audience to share. The more shares, the more authority ranking Google will give your site, and the more potential customers will be visiting.

Google has also introduced Authorship as another way of ranking you online, which allows you to link your online Google+ profile with posts on your website blog. This helps your search engine ranking for your article by assigning a personal validation to it.

When you post an article on your blog and link it to your Google+ profile, your profile photo and number of followers will appear alongside some articles when they are listed in search results. This helps build rapport with your potential customers who have found you through a search, and adds an extra layer of legitimacy to your article or blog post.

Google also measures on-page metrics, which it gathers from its analytics and benchmarking system Google Analytics, such as how long your readers spend reading your article when they land on your site and whether or not someone browses other pages and sections of your site before leaving.

All of this means that it's important to have your content on-message and consistent on your blog and website. If a visitor reads your blog and finds something that doesn't gel with the overall feel of your site, or the link that led them to your article was misleading and wasn't consistent with the content they were expecting, you will be penalised by Google for your content being deemed to be of low quality.

The core principle is that building a compelling online identity is like any other form of communication or marketing—be genuine, sincere and 'real', and if you are, the right customers will be attracted to you.

Google AdWords—reaching people who are trying to find you

Depending on your customer profile, there are probably tens of thousands, if not hundreds of thousands, of people searching for your products and services every month through Google.

Google AdWords allows you to target these people specifically with a brief ad and a call to action.

Your ads can be A/B tested, tracked and improved on a weekly basis to ensure you are reaching the people who are trying to find you and are clicking through to your website.

In setting up your Google AdWords you need to put yourself in the shoes of your customer and ask, 'What are they searching for?' Google AdWords Keyword Planner can help you identify and refine exactly what your customers are searching for, what the search volume is and what the competition level is for each search term.

From there, you need to test and iterate different headlines and ad copy so that you're continually improving the click-throughs to your website, as well as your conversions once the user lands on your site.

AdWords is one of the fastest, cheapest and most effective ways to start building your database and customer base, and making use of it can be implemented immediately.

> To watch a webinar on the step-by-step process of optimising your website using Google AdWords, visit www.unprofessional .com.au/bonuses.

say it world-class fast

Throughout my businesses we have a culture of 'world-class fast', which dictates that everything we do must be world class, and we need to be able to implement quickly.

This is also pertinent when it comes to engaging visitors to your website. You need to be able to tell them why they should use your product or your services, and you need to be able to do this in one short sentence. This is the first sentence I should see when I visit your website.

Let's look at some world-class websites and the first sentence you see when you land on their site:

- *Google Apps*—web-based email, calendar and documents that let you work from anywhere

- *MailChimp*—send better email

- *Dropbox*—your stuff, anywhere

- *Shopify*—design a beautiful online store

- *Evernote*—remember everything

- *Bigcommerce*—get your own store up and running in no time

- *Kogan*—best value LCD TV and LED TV deals in Australia

- *Facebook*—connect with your friends and the world around you

- *Twitter*—find out what's happening right now with people and organisations you care about

- *Wikipedia*—the free encyclopedia that anyone can edit

- *Paypal*—the easy way to pay.

How do you sum up what you do for your customers?

Say it fast

To find your 'world-class fast' message, ask yourself, 'What is the outcome and the benefit we give our customers?' Once you have identified this true reason as to why people use you, fight for brevity and put it into a short sentence.

Creating and implementing a first-class web strategy that reaches out to your market with inspiring and impactful content, having mechanisms to allow people to opt in as easily as possible, and achieving recency and frequency in your communication with your audience will put you in a far more visible position than your competitors. While the professionals are still talking in a sterile language that holds them at arm's length from their customer, forward-thinking small businesses are creating real relationships with their market. You no longer have to use 'corporate speak' in order to appeal to your customer—in fact it's quite the opposite.

Get into the hearts and minds of your consumers, find out what they need to know and *speak* to that. This is what will differentiate your business in today's business world.

Chapter 6

MANAGE AND LEAD

Jack Welch joined General Electric (GE) in 1960. He was employed as a junior chemical engineer on a salary of $10500 per year. In 1961 he began to demonstrate the bold character he would later become famous for, when he tried to walk away from GE because he was unhappy with his suggested pay raise of just $1000 and the bureaucratic nature of the organisation. An executive of GE at the time, Reuben Gutoff, recognised the future potential of someone like Jack Welch and convinced him to stay, on the basis that Gutoff would help create the type of small business environment that Welch was convinced would be more productive for the company.

Twelve years later, Welch would write in his annual performance review that, even back then, it was his goal to one day become the CEO of GE.

In 1981, Welch became GE's youngest chairman and CEO, coming into the role with very clear views about what needed to happen in order to make GE better.

Welch's leadership style throughout his 20-year tenure was seemingly paradoxical: he led the organisation with seemingly contradictory traits. I say seemingly because although from the outside his different approaches may have appeared to be inconsistent with one another, they were in fact part of a very congruent approach to business and leadership—an approach and a philosophy that is arguably one of the best in history.

Welch could appear to be ruthless. His management style was based on brutal candour and straight down the line talk. Often offending or overriding people in meetings or during presentations, he would say it exactly the way he believed it needed to be said—not to offend, but to challenge the thinking of his people and to make them stronger.

Welch would fire the bottom 10 per cent of his employees systematically every single year. He believed wholeheartedly in creating intense competition, and he wasn't interested in working with people who didn't have a competitive instinct.

One of Welch's primary guiding principles was that GE absolutely had to be number one or number two in the industries it played in. He firmly believed that with great people and a competitive culture, to aim for anything less would be not to do his people justice. This resulted in Welch selling and shutting down many of GE's businesses in his early years.

Many of these strategies would later be employed by CEOs and business leaders across the world.

Although on the surface these strategies may seem to be the work of a ruthless leader, Welch's focus on great people and great culture was the centrepiece for his entire leadership strategy from day one.

Speaking with the *Financial Times* in 2008 during the global financial crisis, Welch said:

> On the face of it, shareholder value is the dumbest idea in the world. Shareholder value is a result, not a strategy. Your main constituencies are your employees, your customers and your products.

At the core of Welch's leadership philosophy was not primarily managing for shareholder value, but recruiting, managing and leading great people. Welch knew each of his top 1000 employees at GE by name and was able to comfortably discuss their roles and responsibilities on any given day. He dedicated 50 per cent of his time to the people within GE—training, debating, reprimanding and rewarding.

Each year he gave the top 20 per cent of the employee base bonuses and stock options to reward high performance. Whenever he gave someone a bonus or a stock option, it was never delivered with a letter but rather with a very frank discussion around expectations for the coming year, where he would let the employee know exactly what he expected of them.

He built GE on a culture of informality, essentially tearing down the hierarchical structures that were in place when he first took the seat in 1981. He believed in real human interaction and tried to create a 'coffee pot culture' that encouraged general discussion and debate.

Welch loved the game of business, appreciated great people and had a fierce competitive nature. He loved to reward his top performers while having candid conversations where necessary and making the hard decisions when it was required.

This to me is the essence of leadership: to come from a place of heart and to love the people within and around your organisation, while not shying away from making the hard decisions when nobody else is willing to. Welch no doubt took a 'tough love' approach to leadership.

In 1999 Welch was named the Manager of the Century by *Fortune* magazine, and when he retired in 2001 he had taken the revenues of GE from $26.8 billion to $130 billion. GE had gone from a market value of $14 billion to $410 billion in 2004, making it the largest and most valuable company in the world at the time—the legacy of one of the greatest leaders of all time.

Welch oversaw the GE empire, with hundreds of thousands of employees and hundreds of billions of dollars in revenue, with the decisiveness you would expect to see in a start-up business.

And all of this while still insisting his staff call him Jack.

communicate the vision

Steve Jobs didn't become Steve Jobs by accident. He was very clear about what he wanted to achieve in his life, and the work he was willing to put in, in order to get the job done. Jobs had a vision for his life that was simply 'to make a dent in the universe'. He looked up to iconic figures, such as Albert Einstein, with a vision that one day he would also be considered in the ranks of such historic figures. When he died in October 2011, Jobs was one of the most iconic business leaders of the 21st century.

Apple's success wasn't a coincidence either. The vision for Apple as a company is 'to make insanely good products'. This vision pushes Apple to continually take risks and develop eyes-wide-shut visions of what kind of experience they can deliver through continually creating innovative products. Apple's iPhone, for example, was the highest selling mobile phone in 2008, 2009, 2011, 2012 and 2013.

One of Australia's leading foundations is the National Breast Cancer Foundation. Since the foundation was established in 1994, it has been awarded $97 million to fund research projects across Australia to help those suffering from breast cancer. I'll never forget years ago watching a Breast Cancer Foundation ambassador being interviewed on television and the clarity and conviction that pierced the hearts and minds of everyone in the room as the ambassador proudly stated their ambitious vision of 'ensuring no woman dies of breast cancer as of 2030'.

Great leaders create and communicate grand visions.

 @jackdelosa
Great leaders create and communicate grand visions. #unprofessional

Creating a vision for your life and your organisation can be scary because there is always that little voice in your head that whispers ever so quietly, 'Are you sure you can do all of that?' Regardless of what stage of business you are at, or however successful you become as a person, that voice never goes away. Whether you are Oprah Winfrey, Steve Jobs or Albert Einstein, resistance to your highest purpose will always be there, and the voice that tells you that you can't do it is here to stay. The greats realise this, acknowledge it, and get on with it anyway.

Perhaps even more confronting than creating a compelling vision is communicating it, because now you're accountable. Again, realise it, acknowledge it and continue communicating with absolute confidence regardless.

UNPROFESSIONAL STRATEGIES FOR CREATING A COMPELLING VISION

➤ *Great visions are bold.* They capture people's attention due to the audacious nature of what is being pursued.

➤ *Great visions speak to the heartbeat of the company.* What are you trying to achieve and why is it important?

➤ *Great visions don't carry corporate jargon.* It is not about commercial objectives or using buzzwords, it is about summarising, in one brief and powerful sentence, the audacious goal your organisation is trying to achieve.

As a leader of an organisation your number one role is to amplify the vision of your organisation.

@jackdelosa

As a leader of an organisation, your number one role is to amplify the vision of your organisation. #unprofessional

Once you have set your vision, amplify it. Tell your team, tell your mentors, tell your customers, tell the market, tell the media, tell anyone that will listen. When you think the people around you are sick of hearing about the vision, tell them again.

In today's business world the company that wins is not the company that can act the most professionally or release the best-produced television commercial, it is the company that can create and communicate the most compelling vision that will win the hearts and minds of people everywhere.

build a culture

The Entourage is a place where every morning team members are kicking down the door so they can get in to start work. Each Friday we do Fast Start Friday (Casual Friday isn't in line with the high-performance culture we've created) where everyone starts at 8 am and finishes early for the day at 4.30 pm so we can all have drinks together. We quickly learnt that if we don't remind ourselves to look at our watches, come 6 pm everyone is still strategising, implementing and excitedly working away and we've missed the early finish!

It's an informal, high-performance culture. Talk to any traditional business and they'll tell you that those two words cannot co-exist; talk to any business with a real culture and they'll tell you that those two words, when placed together, empower and excite everybody that sets foot in the office.

SYSTEMS > *PEOPLE* > CULTURE

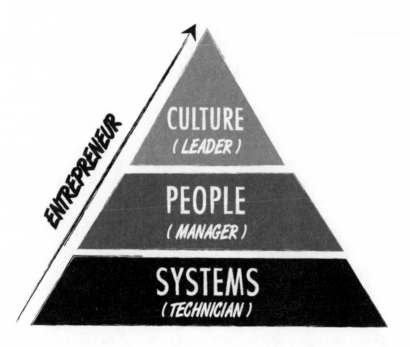

In The Entourage, you can see the vision everywhere, from the hearts and minds of the team, to the posters and quotes on the walls, to the scoreboards that line the walls of every department. Nobody here is working based on a position description; rather, they are working from a genuine pulling sense of self-purpose.

Throughout this chapter we will look at the building blocks of a high-performance culture. Employee empowerment is not about letting people do what they want, but rather setting up the parameters of the game and giving them direction as to how they can best succeed.

In this chapter we will look at the importance of systems, people and how to create great culture.

four steps to creating a captivating culture

You need to follow just four steps to create a captivating culture:

- Create and regularly communicate the vision of the organisation.

- Set non-negotiable standards that you expect everyone in the organisation to meet.

- Ensure everyone knows what the company stands for and the values inherent in the business.

- Show up as the right person. If it is a happy, positive and energetic culture you are building, then every single day, regardless of what's happening at home or in the outside world, you must show up happy, positive and energetic. People look to you for leadership.

set the direction

Once you have set the vision of your company, it's important to set both the medium- and short-term direction. While the vision for the company should be a long-term vision, the direction relates more to specific outcomes that need to be achieved by a certain deadline.

To translate a vision into a set direction requires you to be more specific. This means identifying the key milestones to be achieved for:

- the next two years
- the next 12 months
- quarter by quarter for the next 12 months (0–3 months, 3–6 months, 6–9 months, 9–12 months)
- month by month for the next 12 months.

The balance for any leader is to walk the line between creating the vision and setting the direction, while still ensuring your team has ownership over both. While you are best placed to make the long-term decisions for the business, it is important that you engage your team in the process so that they understand they are an important part of seeing that vision become a reality.

Specifically, as the leader of your organisation you should personally set the milestones that need to be achieved in the next two years and across the next 12 months, and then with your team collaboratively set what the quarterly and monthly milestones need to be in order to achieve the two-year and 12-month milestones. This provides the perfect balance between your providing clear leadership, while engaging your team in helping determine how you can best get there.

become an efficient manager

While leadership is about providing the vision and inspiration to ensure people are engaged, management is about providing the structure to ensure that people understand what is expected of them and how their performance is being measured.

While an effective leader provides energy and direction, an efficient manager provides targets and accountability. As the leader you set the direction; as the manager you enable and monitor performance to ensure everyone is acting in line with the shared objectives.

In my world, leadership is about capturing the hearts of the team, while management is about ensuring we reserve a place in their heads.

As an early-stage business owner, you must become a master of both management and leadership. Eventually you will get to a position where you can afford to employ managers to set up and monitor the processes, which will enable you to focus purely on the leadership side of things, but until then it is critical to the success of your business and the happiness of your people that you do both well. As Stephen Covey says in *The 7 Habits of Highly Effective People*, 'efficient management without effective leadership is like straightening deck chairs on the *Titanic*'.

In 2007, at just 22 years of age, Ben Carroll started a garment printing business as a one-man operation in an underground carpark storage space. Realising that garment printing would soon shift to a digital model, Ben would sit alone in his storage space, cold-calling potential prospects while sitting on a milk crate. Carroll later told *StartupSmart*, an online business magazine, in an interview:

> Black soot from all the exhausts would settle overnight all over everything in the factory. The fumes from our heat presser would create a smoky, steamy room. Each morning, I would have to clean all surfaces to ensure garments weren't soiled during printing. Trying to convince courier drivers there was a business located in the basement was a challenge.

By the time Ben started The Entourage Scalable and Saleable Program in 2011, his company, Velflex, had a small team and worked out of a proper workshop in Sydney, although the business still relied heavily on him. One of the main objectives we set with Ben was to get the business to a point where it could run profitably and successfully without him being involved in the day-to-day operations. Ben recognised there were big opportunities for the business that he simply wouldn't have the time to pursue if his staff needed him to be in the factory every day.

Over just 12 months, Ben documented processes and trained the staff in these systems so that they could effectively operate the workshop without him being there. The company experienced phenomenal growth, but Ben soon realised that he was still the lynchpin when it came to making sales and bringing in new customers. In 2012 Ben brought in an experienced business development manager to take charge of creating partnerships, effectively marketing the brand and bringing in new customers.

Having implemented these strategies of systemising the business, putting position descriptions in place and developing a reporting structure that allowed him to oversee the business from afar, Ben had achieved every entrepreneur's dream of setting up a business that runs without him.

As Ben started to realise the benefits of owning a profitable business, and enjoying the freedom of not needing to be there, he and his fiancée travelled the world together, soaking up as much of the world as they could. The best part was that the business performed just as well when he wasn't there as when he was. In 2011 Velflex was listed as Australia's 25th Fastest Growing StartUp by *StartupSmart*, and today it brings in more than $1.5 million a year. Ben is now exploring further business opportunities with the freedom good management has afforded him.

creating a business that can run without you

Let's explore the four things you need to do to effectively manage a high-growth business and get to the point where it runs without you:

- give them clarity
- manage and monitor
- systematise everything
- get your head in the clouds.

give them clarity

As our business goes through the start-up phase, we tend to hire reactively, bringing in people when we absolutely have to, and perhaps offering them no preparation and minimal training. This is fine: in a start-up business the number one rule is to move fast, so hiring on the fly and bringing people on in an unstructured manner is all part of the game.

As the business grows and roles become more defined, we want to give everybody as much clarity as possible. Confused people do nothing. You want your team to know exactly what is expected of them and what success looks like.

They need absolute clarity when it comes to:

- their roles and responsibilities
- where they sit in the context of the overall organisation
- what characteristics they need to show up to work with
- what is expected of them in terms of performance and targets
- how their performance is being measured
- who they report to and in what format.

We do this by utilising what we call position descriptions. I don't call these job descriptions because I don't want anyone in our businesses acting as if they've got a 'job'. Jobs are dull, boring and uninspiring; I want everyone operating as if they were part of a team and for them to know exactly what position they need to play on that team.

A position description is your opportunity as a manager to create a list of roles, expectations and characteristics that you want this person to embody when they're a part of the team.

Once the position description is created, you can use it during your recruitment process to see which candidates get excited by the role, and as a manager you can use it as a tool to go back to whenever you want to give someone feedback as to what they're doing brilliantly and what you'd like to see them do differently.

Once a person comes on board, they and their manager (this may be you) both sign the position description as an agreement of what everyone is working towards.

Great team members will love thorough position descriptions because it gives them exact clarity over questions that they are probably already asking themselves, questions that in most companies go unanswered. A great team member will love it once they realise what success looks like for them, because it gives them the clarity to pursue success with vigour.

Go to www.unprofessional.com/bonuses to download a position description example and templates for different roles.

manage and monitor

It's important for every manager to have their finger on the pulse when it comes to the performance of the organisation and the people within it. It's also critical for the people within an organisation to understand that they will have a regular opportunity to chat with their manager about their performance, any challenges they may have and whether there is anything else the company can do to best support them.

As we discussed in chapter 4, under the heading 'vital signs and business health' (see p. 76), in order to have crystal clear clarity about what they need to achieve, every person needs to have set targets and objectives that they need to achieve every week, month and quarter. These targets are going to vary depending on the person's role, but the targets should encapsulate the most important components of their role.

However, setting these vital signs is only the first step: we then need to ensure targets are regularly monitored. Because of the fast-paced nature of early-stage businesses, team members will tend to get distracted with projects and tasks that might not necessarily be critical to what their core vital signs are. You therefore need to meet with everybody that reports directly to you, on a weekly basis, for what we call a vital signs chat. Whether the person is in business development, operations or admin, spending 30 minutes with them one-on-one once a week will ensure that they feel heard, valued and supported.

These meetings are about first assessing where the team member is in terms of their weekly targets, and then discussing, in a supportive way, why they believe they're performing well or why they believe they need to improve. If they are exceeding their targets each week then you as a manager want to understand what they are doing and standardise that behaviour across the company. If they're not performing according to the targets they have been set then you need to look at what each of you can do to help them close the gap between where they are and where they need to be.

systemise everything

It should be the objective of every great entrepreneur to build a business that works without them. While you're still stuck in the day-to-day running of the business and management of the team, you can't get out and do what you do best, which is working on the strategic direction of the business, developing partnerships and working on bigger deals that require the broad perspective that only you can bring.

In a start-up business, it may take a while to create a business that can run without you. In the early days, particularly if this is your first business, you will be the person doing everything. You will be the head of digital overseeing the website build, you will be the business development manager who is in charge of sales and marketing, while being the operations manager and the admin assistant before going home at night and being the bookkeeper. However, as you complete all of these tasks every day, you should be asking yourself, what checklist or system do I need to develop in order to one day train somebody else to complete this task?

You might have read books or heard 'experts' say you need to 'fire yourself'. Anyone who has built a business of any real size knows that you don't simply walk into the office one day and 'fire yourself'. It's a long process of systemising, bringing on great people, implementing efficient management structures and providing effective leadership that will allow you to slowly but surely dilute your involvement in the business.

Systemising a business is about getting everything out of your head and getting it written down online, so that other people can complete the tasks that you once did.

Everything that goes on in the day-to-day workings of a business from day one needs to be documented in a step-by-step way so that anybody can step in and conduct that task at the same level of competency that you could. When it comes to sales and business development, you might struggle to find people that can do it as well as you can, so the new rule is that if someone can do it 70 per cent as well as you can, you delegate it.

Anything that happens more than once gets systemised.

@jackdelosa
Anything that happens more than once gets systemised. #unprofessional

In The Entourage, we have systems for every possible task, from opening the office in the morning to visiting the post office, and right up to developing monthly reports for our board meetings. All of these tasks are done seamlessly by members of our team who simply follow the system that has been written for that task.

Our Operations Manual is held in the cloud and runs our business. Having every process and task documented in a step-by-step manner means every team member knows exactly what to do and how to do it. It also means that I, as the business owner, and even our CEO, can be away for months at a time and the business continues to run and thrive as it would if we were in the office.

To me effective systems and implementing good management are about enabling the freedom of the business owner to not be chained to their desk and to the office, allowing them to manage the business from afar, work on more meaningful projects and travel the world when they choose to.

Out of the hundreds of systems that are in our Operations Manual, I personally wrote one: the system for writing systems.

the system for writing systems
Generally speaking, business owners aren't great at writing systems. And while, yes, we do need to be writing systems in the early days when we are still a one-person outfit, ideally when you start to bring on staff, they will start writing and developing systems for the tasks in the business. Particularly

as the organisation grows and your staff start to develop new and better ways of doing things, as well as when more detail comes into the business that you might not even be aware of at an administrative level, it is important that we empower the staff at all levels to write their own systems, and critical that we give them a structure for how to do this.

By providing your team with a system for writing systems, you enable them to develop and update your operations manual as the organisation grows. This also means that each process in the business is written in the same format, which makes it much easier for people to follow when it comes time for team members to follow the system.

The following system for writing systems was shared with me by a great friend of mine, Dale Beaumont. Dale had published 17 best-selling books and launched several successful businesses before the age of 30. His management and attention to detail is impeccable, so I decided to find out how he did it.

HOW THE SYSTEM FOR WRITING SYSTEMS WORKS

➤ **What:** What is being done? This gives the person the overarching context.

➤ **Why:** Why is it important that this task get completed on time and according to the system? This lets the person know what they are doing is important.

➤ **Who:** It is important that here you outline the person's job title and not their name. It is also crucial that one person is responsible for the task and it's not left open for anyone to do. When everyone is responsible, no-one is responsible. Who is accountable to ensure this task gets done?

➤ **When:** What are the trigger points to notify that team member that this task needs to happen? This ensures the person knows exactly when to do this task.

➤ **How:** How is the task or process best implemented? To include in the how:

- a checklist of dot-points of how the task is carried out

- a video demonstration of someone completing the task. If the task is on the computer, then you can use a screen capture video program like Jing or Quicktime; if it is a task that is carried out offline then a simple video recording with a mobile phone is enough.

By following the system for writing systems you not only ensure all of the processes in your business are conveyed and taught in a certain way, but you also ensure that every team member can contribute to the systemisation of the business, freeing you up to work on more meaningful projects.

Visit www.unprofessional.com.au/bonuses to watch a short and sharp interview of me speaking with a technology and systemisation expert about how you can set up your own operations manual in Google Sites.

get your head in the cloud

The only thing worse than having no systems is having systems that are stored separately on everyone's individual computers. The problem with this is that if you've got six staff, you've now got six different systems on six different computers. As people start to improve and update the processes, you will now have conflicting systems on everyone's computer. No longer do we have a unified way of doing things; we are back to the chaos of everyone essentially doing their own thing with little coordination.

A small business is like an orchestra: while everybody has different roles and different instruments, they all need to be playing the same music, being led by the conductor at the front. Otherwise we will be out of tune and off the beat, which results in the audience being turned off.

All systems need to be held centrally, in the cloud, where everyone can view and edit the same system. This means that we don't have duplicate systems and that everyone is playing the same music from the same song sheet.

For this we use Google Sites. This is an online wiki that enables you to set up your systems, categorised by department, updatable by everyone and visible across the company. It means that, for each task, there is just one system, which anyone can access, and anyone with permission can edit the system when an update is needed.

Google Sites also allows you to set different permissions so that some people can only see certain departments. For instance, you might not want everyone in the organisation to see the Finance section, so this section can be made exclusive to you and your accountant. It also means you can set who can edit different systems. One principle we have across our businesses is that anyone can edit a system; however, when they do so, the edit is sent to our operations manager to approve before the change goes live.

As an entrepreneur, you need to get everything out of your head and into a system: how tasks need to be done, the standard that's expected and the policies and principles you want the culture to run on. If you want all of this to be followed across a staff base, it can't just be sitting in your head, which requires you to continually communicate the same things over and over again.

This means that as your organisation grows, you really want to get your head in the cloud.

Chapter 7

KNOW YOUR NUMBERS

Money doesn't need to be scary. In fact, when properly organised, its management not only becomes easy but also enjoyable, as you're able to look through the numbers for your business and understand instantly how much money you're making or losing. As a business owner this is your scoreboard.

When I started out in business at the ripe old age of 18, I didn't know what an invoice was, let alone understand anything about financial management. The idea of 'finance' was something I found overly complex, and I was guilty of not yet appreciating just how important it was for me, as a business owner, to know my numbers.

As my career developed and the businesses I was overseeing grew larger, financial management became crucial to making decisions—when to hire staff; whether we could afford to give someone a pay rise; where we were spending our money and whether some areas could be minimised; what revenue streams were bringing in money and whether they could be maximised; whether we could start to use larger suppliers; and how much we could afford to pay for rent and other expenses. All of these things needed up-to-date and accurate financial information for me to make an informed decision.

What I found was that when I had the right people in the right positions, managing the money of the business became easy.

So often I hear stories of business owners staying up until midnight as they 'do their books', or retailers sitting in their store on a Sunday doing their books on their laptop as customers come in and out of the shop.

> **TIP**
>
> The first rule of finance is that it should be done in collaboration with people who can do it far better than you.

In terms of 'doing your books' (sending invoices, paying staff, paying invoices, reconciling what *should be* in the bank and what *is* in the bank)—all of these functions can be outsourced for as little as $40 an hour. As soon as you get to a point where there is any volume of bookkeeping required, you should be able to outlay a couple of hundred dollars each month on having someone do that job for you while you continue to spend 80 per cent of your time on sales and marketing activities—activities that should be worth a lot more than $40 an hour to the company.

In this chapter, we'll explore the three things you need and the three people you need to manage and monitor your money in a way that is lean and yet gives you absolute clarity, so that you have all of the information you need at your fingertips, at any time of the day and anywhere in the world. This is the new way of doing business.

the business scoreboard

In business, money is the scoreboard. Even if you're not in business primarily to make money, and your 'business' is about pushing your cause or spreading your message, money still needs to be your scoreboard that will underpin your success.

With it, your business, your vision and your message will travel. It will travel through the great people you can afford to employ and motivate; it will resonate through the great partners you can afford to ally yourself with; it will permeate through the media, which will realise you're a credible financial organisation; and it will give confidence to the investors you want to talk to about funding your expansion.

Regardless of what business you are in, or why you are in it, how well you do financially will determine how well you do as an organisation as a whole.

@jackdelosa
Regardless of why you are in business, money will be the underlying scoreboard.
#unprofessional

In business the most dangerous thing you can do is coast from month to month without truly knowing how much money you have made or lost. Some people do this for years, working around the clock on a business that in reality is less profitable than a well-paying job. Not having an accurate financial picture of what they achieve each month means they have little visibility over whether the business is progressing or whether they are simply maintaining the business year to year.

One of the most crucial things to have in business is a financial scorecard—something that tells you every month whether you have gone up or down, and will paint a picture of why you have gone up or down. This not only ensures you can measure your performance against your growth targets, and therefore know whether the business is progressing, but also means you have the information at hand to make important business decisions that will lead to the business developing further.

Not having an accurate and up-to-date financial scoreboard in business that is analysed and discussed monthly is like playing a game of AFL without the goalposts, or a game of rugby without the try line. It means that nobody knows what success looks like, and we have missed the point of the game—players are simply running around getting tired, with no real outcome or objective.

the three things you need

To create a financial scoreboard in an early-stage business is simple, and it can be done in a way that is very lean. Let's look at the three things you need to give you complete financial visibility across your entire business:

- profit and loss statement (P&L)
- balance sheet
- 12-month budget.

We will also look at the three people you need to manage your scoreboard.

profit and loss statement

The vast majority of small businesses in Australia don't know their numbers and have only 'gut feel' as to whether they're making money and, if so, how much.

An up-to-date profit and loss (P&L) statement is the first thing you need to accurately track your numbers. A profit and loss statement is a report that outlines how much income has come in over a given period, such as a month, what your cost of goods was, and what your operating expenses were.

Your P&L looks backwards over a certain period to tell you how the business performed. For instance, a good P&L will allow you to look at how much money you have made or lost over the last month, quarter or year.

A regular monthly P&L statement is critical to knowing whether you're making money, and how much you are making (or losing) each month. It will also allow you to look at which revenue streams are your best, and which expenses are your biggest, which will bring some financial intelligence into your decision-making as a business owner.

By looking at your P&L, and seeing which products or revenue streams are your best, you can then focus more on these. You can see which products aren't performing as well as you would have liked, and you can either look for ways to grow them or, better yet, get rid of them and focus on the products that are higher earners. You can also look at all your costs and see where and what you are spending your money on, so you can work out where you can reduce costs within the business.

At The Entourage, we have developed a business education institution that we believe will be the model of the future for people wanting a real-world business education from people who have 'been there, done that' experience. Our vision is to create a globally recognised institution where people come not only because they want a qualification, but also because they want an education—they want to develop the ability to build a multimillion-dollar company.

In just the last 12 months, from analysing the information on our P&L statements every month, we have stopped delivering some products altogether, shifted the entire business model, redirected all of our focus to the programs that add the most value to our clients and generate the most revenue for the business, and even merged two of our companies. All of these significant decisions, which today mould who we are as an organisation, would not have been made had we not had a meaningful P&L to look at.

@jackdelosa
**Significant shifts in a business model
should be grounded in financial information.**
#unprofessional

Your P&L is also a great gauge of what your customers want, because today consumers vote with their wallets. Your profitable product lines that bring in most of your revenue are the product lines where your consumers are saying, 'We love this. We want more of this.' And they are saying about the product lines that aren't profitable, 'This is not of interest to us. Let's try something else.' Your P&L is the most accurate form of market research that exists, and knowing your numbers means you know your customer.

The good news is you don't need to know how to create a P&L. When we discuss the three people you need to manage your finances, I talk about how these reports are generated and by whom. It is a lot easier and cheaper than you think.

As your business grows, it should be shaped by this financial information. As an entrepreneur, you are an explorer — you are constantly exploring unfamiliar territory for opportunity. As you explore your market, this information should act as a compass, helping you to steer the ship to profitability by the quickest and most effective path. This is not to say you don't innovate and take risks; it is to say that, when you do make the decision to go off course and take risks, you do so in the most informed and calculated way possible. This is the mark of a true entrepreneur.

To see a template of a real-life P&L, visit www.unprofessional.com.au/bonuses.

balance sheet

Your balance sheet is a summary of the assets and liabilities of your business. While your P&L tells you how the business performed month to month, your balance sheet tells you the financial position of the business in terms of what you own and what is owed to you (your assets), versus what you owe to other organisations (your liabilities). These are indicators that are not picked up in your P&L, so it's important to have both in order to gauge the financial health of your business.

The assets on your balance sheet will include things like:

- cash at bank—how much money you have in the bank
- accounts receivable—how much money you are owed by customers
- any property or stock that you currently own.

The liabilities on your balance sheet will include things like:

- accounts payable—how much you owe to suppliers
- employee and tax obligations—how much you owe the tax office in terms of PAYG (pay as you go) withholding tax, income tax and GST
- any loans or debts that the company has.

You can see that, with an accurate P&L showing the financial performance of the business and an up-to-date balance sheet, you can really start to get an insight into the financial health of your business. Using these two things together is critical for effective financial management and will ensure that you always have your finger on the pulse in terms of the financial health of your organisation.

As an explorer, if your P&L is your compass, then your balance sheet is your stock check. The balance sheet shows what you are carrying on your ship in the way of supplies, and what is going to be required on the coming journey. It shows you how much water is on board and how much food you have relative to the size of the ship and crew. Are there enough supplies on board to keep the ship moving in the right direction?

12-month budget

A P&L looks backwards; a balance sheet looks at the present; and a 12-month budget helps you see forward.

A 12-month budget is essentially a projected P&L that looks forward. It is in the same format, with the same line items as your P&L, and it simply outlines what you expect the company to bring in and spend each month for the coming 12 months.

This is critical for any business, because in its absence, the business will simply coast along month by month, not knowing how it is performing relative to the entrepreneur's expectations. Without monthly targets to work towards, it is too easy to get caught in a cycle of non-performance. Every now and again the entrepreneur thinks about the financial performance of the business, but can't really pinpoint whether the company is exceeding or not reaching the targets set.

When you have a well-thought-out budget, every month you have something to measure yourself against. As a business owner, you will inherently lack structure, particularly in the early stage of your business. You don't have a manager looking over your shoulder, checking that you're meeting your targets and asking you questions to help you perform better. As business owners, we need to provide the structure for ourselves. By having a forward-looking 12-month financial budget and measuring it against what you actually achieve every month, you give yourself some much-needed structure that will ensure you ask yourself the right questions about how you can build your business in the most effective way.

As an explorer, your 12-month forward-looking budget is your telescope. Every time you stand on deck and look through your telescope, you can see the forward-looking direction, the condition of the ocean and the point you're aiming for on the horizon. This lets you know what's coming up and how you can best prepare your ship and crew for the seas ahead. With your compass guiding you, regular stock checks to ensure you have enough supplies and your telescope to look forward, you will have everything you need to navigate your ship through both stormy weather and calm seas. Just remember, calm oceans never made a skilful sailor.

> To download a 12-month budget template in Excel format, visit www.unprofessional .com.au/bonuses.

the three people you need

To manage the finances of your business with crystal clear clarity, you only need to have three people in place. These three people will manage your day-to-day accounts, produce the reports and help you make sense of them—all for as little as a couple of hundred dollars per month. Each of these three functions is outsourced, and these people are used only on a needs basis, which means it is relatively inexpensive to have some great people on board doing meaningful work. The three people are:

- the bookkeeper
- the accountant
- the chief financial officer (CFO).

bookkeeper

The first person you need to accurately manage and monitor your finances is a bookkeeper. This person does the administrative and operational tasks that relate to managing the finances of the business.

The roles of a good bookkeeper are:

- producing invoices and receipts for clients
- managing and processing all payments and expenses
- collecting debts
- performing bank reconciliations — making sure everything that is meant to be coming in and going out is actually coming in and going out
- processing payroll according to your pay run period, such as weekly, fortnightly or monthly
- helping with the development of your forward-looking 12-month budget
- extracting regular reports from your accounting software, such as your P&L, balance sheet and business activity statements (BAS).

The bookkeeper is the least senior of the three people you need and current market rates for a good bookkeeper range from $30 to $40 per hour. This is a very wise investment for any business owner to make, because employing a bookkeeper will free them up for hours each month to work on higher value activities.

Go to www.unprofessional.com.au/bonuses to download your bookkeeper position description.

accountant

While your bookkeeper does the day-to-day, week-to-week tasks, they will feed this information and their reports to your accountant, who offers high-level tax and financial advice. Your accountant will also lodge all of your compliance work with the tax office, including your quarterly BAS, PAYG tax and company income tax. If you're not familiar with what these three things are, that's what the accountants are here for.

The roles of a good accountant are:

- assisting in setting up the financial reports, including the structure of the company P&L, balance sheet and forecasts

- projecting and planning for tax payments that will have to be paid and ensure the company manages cash flow in such a way that sees tax payments being made on time

- reporting to management on the financial health of the business

- helping guide the bookkeeper to be as efficient and as effective as possible

- analysing the financial reports to identify where the company can reduce costs without damaging the business or the brand.

Go to www.unprofessional.com.au/bonuses to download an accountant position description.

chief financial officer

Once you have clear bookkeeping in place and an accountant who is effectively managing your tax, you need to engage a part-time chief financial officer (CFO) for a couple of hours per month to talk strategy. A great CFO should bring business and financial experience to the table and be able to help you make better business decisions. While the bookkeeper is an administrative role and the accountant is a compliance and tax role, the CFO is a forward-looking strategic role that is there to help you make smarter financial decisions. That can include when you should bring on staff; how you should remunerate them; whether you should have your own premises; whether you should handle stock or drop-ship straight to your customers; whether you could be paying the bank less money in bank fees each year; whether to raise money from investors; and when and how to expand into new markets. These are all decisions that should be grounded in financial data, and a great CFO should be proactively making these suggestions to you in order to make your business more robust and profitable.

The roles of a good CFO include:

- improving the cash flow of the business by analysing the financial reporting in the business; this may involve reviewing large customer accounts, payment terms, supplier agreements, and inventory and cash management

- assisting in the development of all financial models and reports across the company, helping set benchmarks and key targets for the organisation to achieve; this involves helping you create your vital signs and develop your financial scoreboard

- offering guidance on funding requirements for raising money from investors, and staffing and people efficiency, as well as assisting with strategic business planning at a board level

- advising on the long-term strategy of the business and what the business needs to achieve in order to maximise its value and perhaps even develop a path to exit if you want to sell your business one day; the CFO can help identify the core value drivers in the business and outline how to best enhance these value drivers.

Go to www.unprofessional.com.au/bonuses to download a CFO position description.

this will all change

As your business grows, so too will the ways in which you manage the finances of the company. More importantly, often the accountant or the bookkeeper that you start out with won't be the right person for the job a year or two down the track. As the company grows, you will need to continually find new people whose expertise allows them to stay ahead of the company.

One of the core measures I use to decide whether people are right for the business is based on whether they are driving us or we are driving them. Are we making suggestions to them and guiding them on how it should be done, or are they directing us on how it should be done? The whole point of surrounding yourself with these three people is to ensure that you have people who know more about financial management than you do, and that they can help you stay ahead of the business, proactively planning and putting things in place to ensure the business is as successful as it can be. If your people are simply reacting to what's happening, then it might just be time to find better people.

This is an inevitable part of business. The early stages of a business are so dynamic and change happens so quickly that it is rare for you to find people who will be able to grow at the same rate as the business.

I am fortunate that, after being in business for almost a decade now, I have built my A-team, which is constantly on the front foot and constantly directing me on the best moves to ensure the success of our businesses. But I had to battle through many C-grade and B-grade players before I found the A-grade players.

You to need to build your A-team knowing full well that they may change every now and again as you navigate your way through the early stages of this game called business.

To see who I use to manage our company finances, and why, go to www.unprofessional .com.au/blackbook.

Chapter 8

PLAY THE BIGGER GAME

When I was running my second company, Limitless, in Melbourne at the age of 20 I was achieving relatively good cash flow. After struggling in business for years, I was now making more than enough money to live on and was in a comfortable position for the first time in years. Although I was earning decent money, I started to ask myself questions that I had never asked myself before, big questions that challenged me to think bigger.

Today's equivalent would be questions like these. How does a Janine Allis, someone with no business experience, start Boost Juice with one store in Adelaide and 10 years later sell 65 per cent of it for $70 million? How does a Creel Price and a business partner start a business with $5000, and 10 years later sell it for $109 million? How does a Richard Branson invest $10 million to start Virgin Blue (now Virgin Australia) and list it on the Australian Securities Exchange just three years later for $2.3 billion?

Although I was comfortable, I certainly wasn't yet playing a seven-, eight- or nine-figure game. I wasn't thinking or playing in the realm of millions of dollars, but these people were. They had the same amount of time in the day as everyone else; they didn't come from privileged

139

backgrounds; and they didn't have MBAs or other fancy letters next to their names. So what were they doing differently? I obsessed over this question for years until I found the answer.

The answer, as I discovered it was, like most things, profound in its simplicity. Most business owners view their business as a cash-flow vehicle—something they build as a way of making a couple of hundred thousand dollars each year, running expenses through the business to minimise profit so they can buy more toys and pay less tax. For them it's about going into the business every day, working in the business, maybe growing it, and achieving a bit of cash flow each year.

What was evident when I started to meet with and do business with more high-level entrepreneurs is that, while they recognised that cash flow is critical, they weren't in business to build cash flow: they were in business to build *value*.

These people viewed their business not as a cash-flow vehicle, but as an asset. Like an investment property, a business is an asset that can be built, renovated and maybe even one day sold.

This changed the entire way they went about building their businesses. Rather than working in the business every day, they employed other people to work in the business, allowing themselves to work *on* the business. Rather than trying to become the lynchpin in the business, they ensured systems and processes were set up throughout the business, essentially making themselves redundant, because they realised that the *value* of the business would be so much greater if it wasn't reliant on them.

Rather than simply obsessing about building a great product, they also obsessed about building a great business with asset value that could run profitably without their involvement. Rather than trying to manually win customers every day, they set up partnerships and marketing systems that would see a steady stream of customers come into the business consistently. Rather than minimising their profit to pay less tax, they realised that one of the main value drivers of their business was how profitable the business was, so they would aim to maximise profit every single year, regardless of what this meant from a tax perspective.

Rather than simply growing according to what they could afford, these entrepreneurs would often raise external money from investors to accelerate the growth of their company. Rather than simply thinking about what they needed to do next week, they would also think five years ahead and ask questions like 'Who might one day buy this business?' and 'What does the business need to look like in order for those companies to buy us?'

They played the game of business differently to everyone else. Of course they were thinking about cash flow, but it didn't stop there: they were also thinking *value*.

If you look at the majority of high-net-worth entrepreneurs, their wealth isn't tied to how much cash flow they generated last year—this is just one small driver of business. Their wealth is often tied to the value of their business. In some cases their net worth will be tied to how much cash they have in the bank if they have recently sold a business and now have a good cash position. Their net worth will be based on one of those two things: the value of their business or the value of the business they just sold.

So how do you start playing the game of value? Start thinking of your business as an asset that needs to eventually (perhaps not just yet) run without you.

So far in this book we have examined how to work *on* your business and not *in* it; how to set up your business so it runs without you; how to leverage your marketing through partnerships; how to build recognised brand value in the media; and how to set up a sales system within your company to ensure you maximise your customer numbers. When all of these things are implemented, they will add a significant amount of *value* to your business.

In this chapter we will look at how to raise money from investors, maximise the value of your business even further and position your business for exit, if that's what you'd like to do one day.

raising money from investors

Raising money from external investors can be one way of helping to accelerate the growth of your business. With increasing numbers of investors looking at early-stage businesses, start-up business owners are well placed to create an investment story around the strong growth they expect to achieve.

Today it's incredibly difficult for small businesses to raise money from banks. Often banks will not lend to a business unless it offers them some sort of bricks-and-mortar security, which in a start-up business is often non-existent. This is not necessarily a bad thing, because it means more business owners are starting to look to investors who can add more value than just the money. We call this smart money.

Half the value investors bring to a business should be non-financial, meaning they should also be bringing experience, mentorship and contacts that you can use to grow the business in a faster and more effective way.

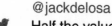
@jackdelosa
Half the value investors bring should be non-financial. #unprofessional

In today's environment, early-stage businesses will typically raise money from sources like colleagues, contacts, high-net-worth individuals, angel investors or sometimes even venture capital firms. When deciding which investors to bring on board, it's critical you think about what ongoing value the investor will bring to the business, aside from just the money.

Companies often raise money for one of two reasons. The first reason is to accelerate growth. More staff, a more aggressive online strategy, a better website that generates more enquiries, a bigger marketing strategy or further product development are all activities that might require external funding in the early stages of business.

Here, raising money is about going to market to create more demand for the business in a bid to build revenues and profitability.

The second reason a company might want to raise money from investors is to facilitate existing growth. Counter-intuitively, growth devours cash and sometimes the faster we grow, the more our cash flow is stretched. For that reason, organisations that are experiencing rapid growth may want to raise money from investors, not to create further demand, but simply to keep up with existing demand. In this case a company might be wanting to invest in more staff, a larger office or warehouse, more cash at bank, more product or stock, a more durable website, or take advantage of opportune buying moments, or perhaps even bring on high level management in a CEO or CFO.

Although there are benefits in raising money, there are also important considerations that you need to take into account before signing up investors.

It's a myth that investors always want to come in and take control and have you working under their direction. My experience and the research show that the vast majority of people who invest in early-stage businesses do not want a controlling stake. Yes, investors in an early-stage play will probably want influence, but most smart investors are going to want to ensure you have a controlling majority stake in the business to ensure you feel motivated to drive the business forward.

Whether you raise money or not should come down to the simple question of: 'What value is raising money going to enable you to create, versus how much value is it going to cost you in equity?'

For instance, if you wanted to raise $200 000 from a private investor, but you could only justify a valuation of the business of $400 000 (we'll talk about how to value your company in the section on p. 152, under the heading 'how to value your business'), then the capital raising is going to cost you 50 per cent of your business. In this case, you need to seriously consider two things:

- Are you comfortable with that sort of dilution of ownership? Not taking the money means the business will probably take longer to build, but you will keep a larger share of ownership.
- What other value does this person or company bring to the table? What ongoing value will they provide?

To make a decision, consider two scenarios in which you project (guess) what is going to happen. Scenario A sees you raising the money, while Scenario B sees you growing organically without raising funds. In five years time, or at the point of exit, which do you think will be more valuable: 50 per cent ownership in Scenario A or 100 per cent ownership in Scenario B?

In another instance, if you work out you need to raise only $100 000 and you can defend a valuation of $800 000, meaning you will be giving up 12.5 per cent in equity in exchange for the investment, and you were confident that doing so would enable the business to reach a valuation of $2 million in two years, then this would be a more attractive proposition for you as the business owner.

When you are considering whether you should raise money (see table 8.1), consider these formulas:

- you know what you want to do with the money + you have proof of concept + it will add more value to you in the long term than what it will cost in equity = good reason to raise money

- you're not quite sure what you're going to do with the money + the concept or model is not yet proven + it will cost me too much in equity = good reason *not* to raise money.

Table 8.1: deciding whether to raise money

	Unclear use of funds	Clear use of funds
Proof of concept achieved	You may be successful in raising a small amount of capital.	Good investment opportunity for investors.
No proof of concept	Do not raise money until you have determined the use of the funds and achieved relative proof of concept.	You may raise money but it will be at a low valuation.

Whether you raise money from investors or not is as much a personal decision as it is a commercial decision. Some people operate with the belief that you should always bring in external money; some people are against it, saying start-ups are better when they're short of cash. The reality is that the situation is different for every business and for every person.

If you want to engage smart money and have experienced people financially invested in your business, then capital raising may achieve that. However, if you want to go it alone and don't want to have other shareholders at the table, then that is what you need to do. The good news is that you have a choice.

three questions on every investor's mind

Every investor wants to see a great return on their investment in any business they go into. Although this is usually an investor's main priority, it is not what they look for first as investors. What they look for in any potential investment is the risk.

Intelligent investors will often work on the basis of null hypothesis, which is to say that every idea is a bad idea until proven otherwise. In the investor's world, every potential investment is a bad investment until proven otherwise. For the entrepreneur, that means you need to know how to lower the investor's resistance before you can start trying to build their acceptance and paint the blue sky opportunity.

Most smart investors are asking themselves three distinct questions, and in a very particular order, every time they assess an opportunity. Understanding these questions and in which order to address them is the key to a good pitch.

THREE QUESTIONS INVESTORS ASK THEMSELVES

---

1 Am I going to lose my money?

2 When am I likely to get my money back?

3 Am I likely to make any money?

The main problem is that most people looking for an investor jump straight to addressing question 3 before addressing questions 1 and 2.

Investors are cautious by nature. They have made a lot of money, but they have also lost a lot of money and can see all the red flags that pop up when an optimistic entrepreneur is on the front foot.

Let's look into the specifics of each question.

am I going to lose my money?

The investor will be thinking:

- What is the experience of the entrepreneur?

- Has the entrepreneur engaged mentors and advisers who have significant industry and business experience?

- To what degree has the business achieved proof of concept?

when am I likely to get my money back?

The investor will be thinking:

- Is there a clearly defined exit strategy for the entrepreneur?

- What companies are likely to buy this business?

- What is the time line to exit and how committed to the exit is the entrepreneur?

am I likely to make any money?

The investor will be thinking:

- What are the milestones achieved to date?

- Where is the growth path for this business?

- Who are the companies that might one day buy this business?

If you can tick each of these boxes through thorough preparation and a calculated pitch, you will be well on your way to getting the interest of the investor.

why value matters

An entrepreneur's unrealistic expectation of valuation of their company is the number one problem that stops investors from investing. Too often the entrepreneur does not understand how to professionally value a business or, if they do, can create a valuation that is overly optimistic.

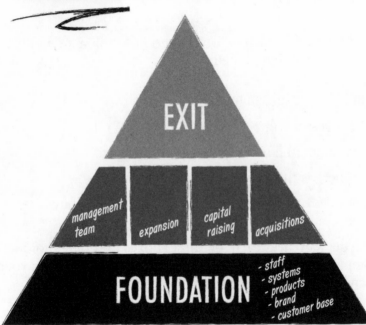

We have already established that high-level entrepreneurs and the world's wealthiest people are first and foremost concerned with the *value* of their business and continually increasing the value of the asset. Therefore, it's important for any entrepreneur at any stage of the game to understand what the different drivers of value are in the business world.

The traditional and most common way of valuing a business is through calculating a multiple of profits.

 @jackdelosa

The traditional and most common way of valuing a business is through a multiple of profits. #unprofessional

The average multiple of private businesses in Australia generally fluctuates around two times net profit before tax. It's important to realise that this is the *average* multiple; educated business owners should always aim for a valuation of at least four times profit before tax.

It is not unrealistic to expect a significantly higher multiple than four if you have a durable business and understand how to structure a capital raising. For my own businesses, such as MBE Education and The Entourage, we have raised money from investors by valuing the company at a multiple anywhere between eight and 16 times net profit. How? By having a thorough understanding of what drives value and being able to communicate a strong growth story to incoming investors.

Often, start-up businesses have no profit to multiply. In this case the owner needs to create assumptions about the future and multiply the projected profit, or look at what the non-financial value in the business may be one, two or three years from now. This only strengthens the need to make the future real by providing proof of concept, consumer insight, market trends and any evidence that supports the assumptions they're making.

Let's look at how to determine what multiple is right for your business.

how to value your business

There are 10 valuation drivers that investors or potential acquirers are going to look at in order to determine the multiple, and therefore the value, of your business. Understanding each of these, and being conscious of working on them across the life of the business, will hold you in good stead in ensuring you achieve the highest possible valuation of your business.

the 10 valuation drivers of business

- *Proof of concept.* How proven is it that people are buying (or will buy) from you, and will continue to buy from you?

- *Cash flow and profitability.* Does the business have smooth cash flows and reliable profitability?

- *Customer base.* Does the business have a loyal customer base, have a database of customers and strong repeat business?

- *People.* How established and capable is the team within the business?

- *Key-person dependence.* How reliant is the business on one or two key people (usually the founder or founders)?

- *Systems and reporting.* How systemised are the operations of the business, and how well does key information float up to key decisionmakers?

- *Brand.* How strong is the brand and the media presence of the business?

- *Governance.* From a legal and financial perspective, does the company have all the necessary contracts in place with suppliers, staff and partners, and is the company operating responsibly with its finances, with all taxes and liabilities being paid to date?

- *Growth potential.* Is the profitability or value of the business, or both, likely to increase significantly and offer investors or acquirers the uplift they need to see a return on investment?

- *Strategic value.* Who could monetise this business to a further extent than the current owners, and are they likely to one day want to purchase this business?

How well you're able to prepare and achieve each of these 10 points will determine what sort of multiple you're able to defend to investors. Table 8.2 shows some indicative multiples for different stages of development within your business.

Table 8.2: multiple guide for an existing business

Multiple	Explanation	Vehicle
Over 10	Business has significant strategic value to another company or investor, meaning someone else can make more money from this business than you can, as the founder and current owner, so it is worth more to them and they are happy to pay a premium. This strategic value is real and is recognised by a potential investor or acquirer.	Strategic asset
8	Exceptional business with very reliable cash flows, customer base and profitability. Net profit before tax probably exceeds $4 million. Run under management with the business owner/founder simply taking a board role. Strong operational reporting and clear financial reporting. Great brand in the industry, with strong potential to grow the brand even further. Proven business model that could be replicated in other states, countries or markets.	Asset
4	Solid business with good cash flow, established business model, good systems, strong team, still reliant on the business owner to be involved operationally, but dependence is minimal. Good and loyal customer base so future earnings are somewhat protected, good brand with potential to boost the brand further, strong growth potential with more marketing and business development activities, and operating in a strong market or growth sector.	Business

(continued)

Table 8.2: *(cont'd)*

Multiple	Explanation	Vehicle
2	Average business that is quite reliant on the day-to-day involvement of the business owner. Systems are quite weak, clients aren't contracted in, few or no recurring revenue streams, not much brand awareness beyond the existing customer base, plateaued or minimal year-on-year growth.	Self-employment
1	One-person consultancy; if the business is ever sold the acquirer won't be buying an asset, they will be buying a job.	Job

Although a multiple of profits is the most common way to value a business, sometimes if a business doesn't have profits or if there is something within the business that is more valuable than the profit, such as the database, a product that can be scaled or some IP that is highly valuable, then we can look at the strategic value of the business and this will often allow us to reach an even higher valuation.

strategic value

In October of 2007, Microsoft invested in Facebook to the tune of $240 million. For their investment Microsoft now owned 1.6 per cent of the global social networking company, giving Facebook a value of around $15 billion. At the time, Facebook was losing approximately $1 million per month.

How do companies like Facebook, some of which are losing money, achieve such high valuations?

It comes down to strategic value—the hidden value that lies within every business.

A number of years ago we were working with a magazine to help the business raise money from investors. It was a good magazine that was well known in its industry, and it wanted some extra capital to help accelerate its growth plans. We quickly identified that if we were to value the magazine using the traditional multiple of profits methodology, then we wouldn't be doing the magazine justice as the profit was still quite low. We needed to find a different way to value the business: we needed to find something else of value within the business that wasn't its profit.

The magazine had a database of 40000, which is a strong asset in itself, so we decided to survey the database to get more information about the people who were on this database. With a quick email survey, incentivised with some digital gifts for anyone who participated, we were able to collect some very important information, which was later crucial in putting forward a favourable valuation to investors.

The most impactful finding of the survey was that 40 per cent of the 40000 people on the database owned property. Not only that, but of the 40 per cent who owned property, half indicated that their number one investment decision over the next 12 months was going to be to purchase an investment property.

Suddenly, with a quick email survey to the company's database, we had identified that 8000 readers who owned a property and therefore had income, serviceability and probably equity in their existing property, also indicated that they would like to purchase an investment property in the next 12 months.

Let's say you're a property developer and you make $10000 per property that you sell. We have a magazine with a database of 40000 people, 8000 of whom own property and want to buy another one within the next 12 months.

Is this business now worth significantly more to you as a property developer than the profit that we achieved in the last 12 months?

Absolutely it is. That's strategic value.

> **TIP**
>
> Strategic value is about identifying the non-financial value in your business and carefully selecting *who* it will represent value to.

To identify the strategic value in any business, simply ask yourself one question: 'Who could make more money from this business than I can, and why?'

>
>
> Strategic value is about asking 'who could make more money from this business than I can and why?' #unprofessional

The strategic value is going to be different in every business and might include:

- *Database*. As in the magazine example, someone can make more money from the database than you can, and so they would be happy to pay a higher price to become an investor.

- *Product or service*. You're currently selling a proven product to an audience of a few thousand customers, but a potential acquirer could sell this product through their distribution of hundreds of thousands of customers through their global distribution network.

- *Intellectual property*. The business owns some sort of protected intellectual property (IP), such as purpose-built software, a licence or a new investment that another company can monetise to a greater extent than you can.

- *Niche*. You are a market leader in a particular niche that another business wants to access, and it is easier for them to invest in you and even one day acquire you than to start from scratch.

- *Brand*. There is significant brand equity in your business and this is valuable to a potential investor or acquirer.

If you can identify the strategic value in your business and how you can begin to maximise that value, then when it comes time to raise money from investors or sell your business, you're going to be able to achieve a much higher valuation than if you were to simply value the business as a multiple of profits.

know the process of raising money

Most entrepreneurs who seek money from investors never get it. There are a number of reasons for this, but most of it comes down to the entrepreneur not being educated on how to structure and implement a successful capital raising.

Raising money is like every other facet of business — it is a skill, and that means it can be learned. It takes time to fully understand how to raise money, and some people do it far better than others.

The ones that do succeed in raising money have a great combination of a good business, a strong growth story and a well-executed process for raising the money.

Let's look at a 10-step process you can follow to successfully raise money from investors.

The 10 steps to raising money from investors

Following these 10 steps gives you a clear process for raising money from investors.

1 create the offer

Set the parameters of the deal:

- Place a desired valuation on the business, understanding that the investor will negotiate this value down.
- Decide how much money you will try to raise.

- Determine what the money will be spent on and the projected return from these activities.

2 build your team

In order to implement a successful capital raising you will need several people in your corner:

- An experienced entrepreneur who can advise you on the strategy of the capital raising, how to best structure the offer and how you should handle the negotiation process.

- A solicitor who can help you with all the legal considerations, documents and processes that legislation requires you to follow.

- A financial adviser who can help you tidy up any financial information you have, put together a forward-looking financial forecast and advise on any financial considerations.

3 prepare the business

Become investor-ready by addressing these three aspects of your strategy:

- Ensure the growth strategy is researched and decided upon.

- Ensure the business has been de-risked from a legal and financial perspective, with all company contracts up to date and all financial information in place.

- Ensure current business performance is favourable and the important numbers are trending up.

4 create the documentation

To successfully raise money you will need three documents:

- *Information memorandum (IM)*. This is a relatively short document (20–30 pages) that outlines the investment highlights, potential risks and the offer.

- *Executive summary*. This is your one-page marketing flyer, which should summarise the IM. This is the document that you would send to potential investors or give to them during initial conversations to give the investor the opportunity to read something very brief and decide whether it's an opportunity they would like to learn more about.

- *Pitch presentation*. This is essentially your IM in pitch presentation format. Make the structure and subheadings the same as your IM, but include less body text, as you or your adviser will talk investors through the presentation.

> Go to www.unprofessional.com.au/bonuses to see a video of me outlining the exact structure of an information memorandum and executive summary.

5 approach investors to gauge interest

Send a brief email with the executive summary attached to:

- your personal networks
- angel investors and venture capital investors
- any high-net-worth individuals who may be interested in your industry and business.

TYPES OF INVESTORS

Investors can be described in a number of ways. Here are definitions of the two main types you will hear about.

> ➤ *Angel investor*. Typically an individual who has experience or interest in your particular industry. Can be flexible and creative with their investments, as they

are not bound by the same rules professional funds are. Ideal investor for early-stage businesses.

➤ *Venture capital investor.* A professional investment firm that has to invest according to their investment mandate. These investors are investing other people's money, so they have less flexibility in their investment approach. It's good to speak to targeted VCs once the company is more established.

---

6 host investor information evening(s)

Host a small and intimate event with potential investors to give them more information about the deal. The investor information evening should include three facets:

- A 20-minute presentation by you or your adviser on the offer. If you are comfortable with the details of the capital raising you can do this yourself, or you can engage an adviser who can better communicate the growth path of the business and the investment offer if you prefer. This is where you will use the pitch presentation you developed in step 4, and even demonstrate your product or service however you can.

- A 15-minute Q&A that gives the audience an opportunity to ask questions of you and your adviser.

- A call to action for anyone who is interested to complete an expression of interest. Anyone who completes an expression of interest (which does not oblige them to invest but simply indicates that they are interested in exploring the opportunity further) will get a full information memorandum to take home and discuss with their advisers.

7 hold meetings with potential investors

Now that your potential investors have learned about the offer, those who want to explore it further will most likely ask to meet you and any other owners of the business. For these meetings it is important that you:

- Prepare. Have all of your documentation and financials ready.

- Be completely open, honest and willing to acknowledge the downside risk, while being confident in your own ability and the growth of the business.

- Be prepared for the potential investor to request more information and go through their own due diligence.

8 due diligence

This is where the investor will want to go through the business in detail to verify everything you have presented and look for holes in the business, your assumptions and the plans. The investor will do three types of due diligence:

- *Commercial due diligence.* Working out how likely the business is to make money, attract more customers and grow at the rate you're projecting.

- *Financial due diligence.* Looking through the financials of the business to ensure that they match the story that has been presented. The investor may also go through the forward-looking forecasts to see if they are sound. Here the investor will also look to see whether the company is up-to-date with the payment of its liabilities, such as tax, superannuation and creditors.

- *Legal due diligence.* Reviewing the contracts the company has with its employees, suppliers, shareholders, board members, customers, partners and any other parties. The investor will also look at whether the company is or has been involved in any legal disputes.

9 settlement

Now the investor gets their shares and the company receives the money. This process should be facilitated by a solicitor and will involve, but not be limited to, the completion and signing of:

- a capital raising application form

- a shareholder's agreement, which outlines the rules of how all the shareholders are going to operate and how decisions will be made

- share certificates that signify who owns shares and how many they own.

10 investor management

Now that the investors are on board, the hard work begins. You now need to deliver on the growth story you have presented. To keep investors up to date with all developments, both good and bad, ensure you do three things:

- *Communicate with them as developments arise.* If they are board members then you should have a monthly board meeting. If they are not board members, then a simple email update when anything significant happens is always appreciated.

- *Deliver a formal quarterly investor update.* This outlines all the performance metrics and results of the last quarter and gives an overview of the updated plans.

- *Hold an annual general meeting (AGM).* This is a meeting for all shareholders, where you and any other key personnel present the last financial year's results and your plans for the coming year(s). AGMs are usually held in August, after a company has had time to reconcile its accounts and digest its performance over the last financial year (July–June).

your ultimate payday (maybe)

When Dean McEvoy and Justus Hammer started Spreets, a group-buying platform based in Sydney, they did so wanting to build the business quickly, and then exit.

Seeing that group buying was a model that had worked well in the United States with businesses like Groupon, Dean and Justus recognised that this was a model that had low barriers to entry and would attract a number of players, so, once they had proved the model worked in the Australian market, they raised money from investors to accelerate their growth and reach a position of market leadership.

After kicking off in Sydney, they proved the model in a way that was very lean and involved Dean personally calling potential companies to list deals. They then raised money to accelerate growth, surrounding themselves with their A-team (partnering with a great incubator called Pollenizer), and sold Spreets to Yahoo!7 for $40 million just 10 months after they started the business.

Speaking with Dean after the sale, I learned that, while all of this had happened in 10 months, Dean had been trying to launch other start-ups for the last seven years, and had learned a lot through the challenges he had faced in his previous businesses. They had formed Dean's apprenticeship. He was a genuinely humble, very respectable and grounded entrepreneur. In Dean's words, taken from our 2011 interview on YouTube, it's not about trying to raise money or trying to build a business to sell, but rather 'just try to build something that's fascinating, interesting and compelling that people just want to be involved with'. Raising money and perhaps an ultimate exit will be a side effect of building something great.

I agree with this approach. While you should have one eye on the long-term strategy of your business and what the potential exit might be, business is first and foremost about building something great. Once you have done that, offers from investors who want to invest and acquirers who want to buy your business will start to find their way across your desk. At this point you have the choice of whether to sell or not to sell.

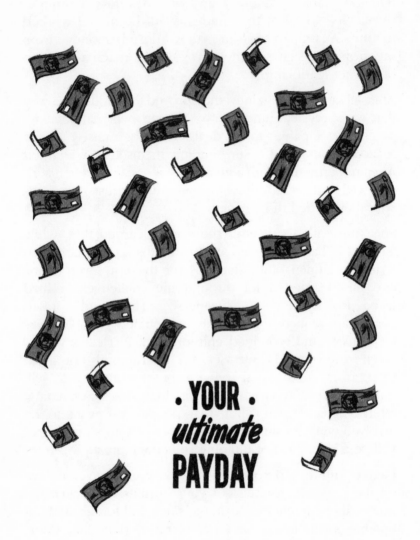

Yes, when you sell your business that will be your big payday. That's where you cash in on the kind of money that you can retire on, or the kind of money that will allow you to invest in other businesses. However, some people don't wish to sell their business any time soon, because for them it is a process of creating something they're proud of and seeing how much of an impact they can make. Both approaches are completely fine and it comes back to the question, 'Why are you in business?'

That is a question only you can answer.

If you do one day want to sell your business for the highest possible price, then let's make sure you maximise the opportunity by doing it right.

positioning your business for exit

As a business owner, the most valuable asset you own should be your business. After you have started a business and built it into an asset with value, you need to know how to extract the value in the best possible way.

Too many business owners spend 20 years building a business, only to shut it down when they retire because they don't understand how to position a business for exit. They have worked their entire life, put their heart into their business, and never fully realised the return they could have or should have generated for themselves and their family.

There are three fundamentals to positioning your business for exit. Following these fundamental elements will ensure that your business is best prepared for sale and that you achieve the highest possible price.

- *Identify potential buyers.* The value of your business will depend entirely on what it is worth to someone else. This is about identifying the strategic value in the business and again asking yourself, 'Who can make more money from this business than I can?' Even if the sale is 10 years away, start building a relationship with these businesses straight away so that they get to know you and your business.

- *Become sale-ready and maximise your valuation.* For this, refer to the steps we spoke about in the previous section the 10 valuation drivers of business'. Whether you're boosting your valuation to raise money from investors or to sell the business, the preparation process is very similar.

- *Create competitive tension.* Six to 12 months out from the sale date, engage with four or five potential acquirers who are all interested in purchasing your business. The more potential acquirers you have in the sale process, the higher the valuation you will achieve. It's no different from a property auction: you want to have as many bidders interested as possible.

World-class entrepreneurs view business not solely as a vehicle to generate cash flow, but rather as a vehicle to build significant value. Throughout *UnProfessional* we have looked at each of the different considerations for growing your business in a way that outperforms larger businesses, and in this chapter we have examined how you can take that growth and build on the solid foundation in order to engage investors, if you want to, but more importantly to start building real value into this asset that is your business.

Approaching business in this way and building a business that can work without you is what will differentiate your business and you as an entrepreneur from all the other players out there.

Welcome to the 1 per cent.

Chapter 9

IT'S YOUR REVOLUTION

To me, entrepreneurship is the highest form of self-expression and the greatest enabler of freedom we have. To have the ability to choose what you want to build and consciously create something of value that matters to other people and improves their lives is one of the most noble endeavours a person can take on. The challenges, obstacles and inevitable setbacks you will encounter along the way only act to make it all the more admirable.

At 10.35 am on 17 December 1903, Orville Wright, after winning a coin toss with his brother, launched 'the first sustained and controlled heavier-than-air, powered flight' in a paddock called Kill Devil Hills in North Carolina, USA.

This moment in history is significant for a number of reasons.

First, neither Orville nor his brother Wilbur had finished high school, let alone gone on to complete tertiary studies. The people that the Wright brothers were competing against for aviation history not only had electrical engineering and mechanical engineering qualifications, they also had access to capital—another luxury not afforded to the Wright brothers.

Second, this first sustained and controlled flight was quite a humble moment relative to today's standards. Orville travelled just 37 metres in 12 seconds at a speed of only 10.9 km/h. The brothers who are today recognised as the fathers of modern-day aviation started with a small flight of just 37 metres. Regardless of the footprint you end up leaving on the world, in the first instance your accomplishments will be insignificant — particularly when they are compared with your visions of what is possible.

And, lastly, the events of this day are significant because the Wright brothers did not have a pilot's licence; they weren't accredited by an aviation body, qualified as pilots or recognised as leaders in their field. How could they be? The path they were forging had not been walked before. The industry they were creating did not yet exist.

The great thing with the world today is that, so long as you are adding value to people's lives and changing the world for the better, people often won't care whether you have a formal qualification. Your qualifications in business are the results you can produce for your customers.

In business, there is a gap. There is a gap between how well we think we should be performing, or how big we think we should be, and where we are today. Regardless of how grand your vision, how audacious your goal, when you start something new, you will not be great. In fact you will probably not be very good at all. Remember, in your first attempt you are not trying to build an aircraft that will carry hundreds of passengers across vast oceans to far away destinations; you simply need to fly 37 metres. Start before you're ready and realise that you will probably start small and stay small for a while.

And, finally, don't wait for permission. Your licence in business is your ambition to dream of things that never were and your courage to give it a try. Your currency is how much value you can deliver to your customers and to what extent you can enrich the lives of your team. Permission is granted to you only by your willingness to accept temporary failure in the pursuit of ultimate success.

Don't let anyone, especially the professionals, tell you any different. This is your revolution.

INDEX

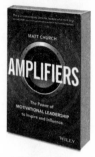

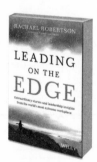

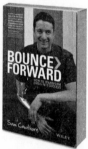

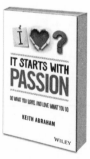